IF LIFE GAVE ME
LEMONS,
I WOULD TURN IT INTO
HONEY

Based on a Life Story

ANNE-MARIE K. KITTIPHANH

Order this book online at www.trafford.com
or email orders@trafford.com

Most Trafford titles are also available at major online book retailers.

Printed in the United States of America.

ISBN: 978-1-4669-9604-5 (sc)
ISBN: 978-1-4669-9606-9 (hc)
ISBN: 978-1-4669-9605-2 (e)

Library of Congress Control Number: 2013909817

Trafford rev. 06/04/2013

 www.trafford.com

North America & international
toll-free: 1 888 232 4444 (USA & Canada)
phone: 250 383 6864 ♦ fax: 812 355 4082

Contents

To My Family

~~~~~~~~~~

For Always Being There

&

The Doctors & Nurses
That Treated Me @

~~~~~~~~~~~~~~~~

Saint Michael's Hospital
The Hospital For Sick Children
Make-A-Wish Foundation
&
Bloorview Macmillian Rehabilitation Centre

If Life Gave Me Lemons, I Would turn It Into Honey
Inspired By A Backstreet Boy
(He Is Mentioned In The Story)

What Lupus (*Systemic Lupus Erythematosus*) SLE Is

I know that people always ask, what is lupus (SLE)? to me I think it is just a disease that involves your immune system and also your blood, lots of medication, lots of blood work, and also lots of doctors' appointments. There are other things that involve lupus as well, but I can't remember everything that was told to me. All I know is that it is a life-threatening disease—a disease that I almost died from. I persevered through everything & made everything into something positive, I was always bubbly and happy, even though I was in a certain situation that was very unsettling, I always made everyone smile. I may have been in a hospital for a life threatening illness but I am always smiling, even in the toughest times of my disease, I always had a smile on my face to make everyone, even myself feel better, that is the only thing that helped me get through—other than my mom and my favorite music but mostly having complete strangers give up some of their blood to save someone's life such as mine, I had about forty or more blood trans-fusions to help keep me alive, I am thankful for whoever has the B+ blood type. The rarest blood type is one that is not available when a child needs it. Therefore, it is essential for The Children's Hospital to have donors available who represent all of the four blood types: O, A, B, AB. Each of the four blood types has either a positive or negative Rh factor. Blood types O and A are the most common and must be replenished daily. Groups B and AB are rarer and collected as needed.

Rh Blood Type	How Many Have It?	Frequency in the U.S.	Who can receive my bloodtype?	What Blood type can I receive?
O +	1 person in 3	37.4%	O, A, B, AB	O Pos/Neg
O -	1 in 15	6.6%	O, A, B, AB	O Neg
A +	1 in 3	35.7%	A, AB	A & O Pos/Neg
A -	1 in 16	6.3%	A, AB	A & O Neg
B +	1 in 12	8.5%	B, AB	B & O Pos/Neg
B -	1 in 67	1.5 %	B, AB	B & O Neg
AB +	1 in 29	3.4%	AB	AB & O Pos/Neg
AB -	1 in 167	0.6%	AB	AB & O Neg

Intro & Jamie's Accident

All the classes in Holy Family School were in session, it was nearing the end of the day. Mr. C's Grade 7 & 8 students were heading for physical education. There are 21 students in the class among them is me Anne-Marie Kittiphanh fifteen yrs old, black hair, brown eyes & glasses I weighed 100 pounds and I respond to either Anne-Marie or Annie—mostly Annie.

I had went to the same school since kindergarten. Now I was in seventh grade, getting changed for physical education. I had completed all. Between attending two elementary schools, they were Andrew Hunter and Saint Nicholas I had passed grade 7 and would begin my High School classes in Englehart, where I was staying with a family friend Jane.

I would always return to Englehart because it's small & everybody knew everybody, the teachers & students in Holy Family knew my family and me. Along with Jane, being a close family friend, she was almost like a second mother to me and my brothers. I felt comfortable with Jane.

The reason I would always return was school. The only people I knew I & my family could trust was Jane & her family, whenever I traveled south I would always stay in contact with Jane.

Since I was still in seventh grade I decided to enroll & finish that grade level at Holy Family. I enjoyed myself for the most part until I received news of a family emergency. I had just finished changing and headed out to the main hallway toward the gym. As I stepped out of the girls' change room, I noticed my teacher, Mr. C with a grim expression on his face.

He looked at me and said, "*I just received a message from Jane, you need to get home right away.*" I felt a little confused I asked "*What is it about?*",

"*Just go home, you will find out*" was all he said, so I turned and headed back to get my regular clothes. I decided to just wear them over my gym clothes.

I grabbed everything including my homework. What was happening? Was it my family? I went straight home. Jane was waiting for me in her cozy bungalow.

I looked over at Jane, and asked "*What's wrong?*" I saw the same grim expression

Jane said "*It's your brother Jamie. He was in a car accident*"

"*My wonderful older brother was in a car accident?*"

I heard Jane say "*Yes*" and I collapsed, in tears.

I stopped crying long enough to ask "*Can I call my mom?*"

Jane nodded. She dialed my mom's phone number for me.

(On the phone)

"*Mom, I love you,*" I sobbed
"*Annie*" said my mom "*we are arranging for
Jane to bring you to Sunnybrook Hospital
in Toronto*" "*Okay,*" I said. "*Will Jamie
be okay?*"
My mom's voice shook. "*We don't know yet,*"
she said.

(End of Phone call)

After I spoke to my mom on the phone, I let out another batch of tears. Jane had known my entire family since my brothers & I were born, we were like a big family, and when I moved away I would always keep in contact with Jane because I missed her.

I even sent letters back & forth with Jane. She was there for me whenever I needed someone. Whenever I would to Englehart for a visit, I would stay with Jane. When I moved away I was in third grade I miss my old school because I was known there.

I had been going back & forth between wherever my family was and staying with Jane for two and a half years. By the time I got to the eighth grade level, I chose to stay with Jane.

I sat with Jane as I let out my tears. Soon after, I went to pack my clothes before we got picked up to head to SunnyBrook Hospital in Toronto.

My brother was flown to SunnyBrook after being pulled out of the vehicle he was in. Once we all got picked up, all

I couldn't stop crying and going in & out of sleep 'cause of knowing my brother was in an accident. Once we all made it to the hospital we headed to the waiting room of the intensive care unit, located on the second floor where my family was waiting. As soon as we got in, I walked right into my mom's arms and cried once more. I noticed my oldest brother, Bob, in one of the comfy chairs, and my mom's boyfriend standing a few feet away.

After I finished crying I was able to calm down enough to ask *"Can I go in & see Jamie?"* my mom said *"Yeah, Bob will go in with you"*, I went with Bob to see Jamie in the intensive care unit room we had to go through two different doors before locating where Jamie was. We found him in the fourth bed with a cast on his left arm and a wrap around his head, the head injury that he sustained put him in a coma.

The accident itself wasn't far from the Barrie local hospital, Royal Victoria he was brought in where he lost consciousness & found out that he received a head injury so he was emergency flown to Sunny Brook in Toronto. When we went to see Jamie he looked like he were in a deep sleep, Bob & I each went to stand on either side of the bed not able to say anything.

I found out later that my mom had rented a motel room across the street from the Hospital, so I, my mom & Jane went there to rest for the night. The next day I found out from my mom that my dad was going to be arriving at the hospital to see my brother, I never got to see my dad until I got to the Hospital.

I was able to spend some time with my dad who was dressed in orange monk robes (part of Buddhist Religion), along with visit Jamie again after a while. After spending time with my dad I noticed the Driver of the Car Accident came to see Jamie, the guy came to the waiting room and I stood up in a defensive stance and asked "*So what do you think?*" only to be pulled back by my mom who said "*Annie!*" in a warning tone, I looked at my mom and made a face saying '*what? He almost killed my brother don't expect me to be nice to him*' kind of look, I felt upset & angry with the driver who happened to be Jamie's friend.

I had a right to feel upset because I found out later that the joyride was the Driver's idea, it was during a school day and all had time to spare they figured why not. Problem was that during the joyride he began yelling out a threat—which was close to being real—to all who were lucky to be alive.

The threat that was yelled was "I'm going to kill you all. You're all going to die!". He may have meant it as a joke except he somehow lost control of the vehicle swerved across the pavement and hit a hydro-pole (location of the Car Accident was on Penetanguishene Road). Jamie was the passenger sitting behind the Driver, there was another passenger sitting behind the passenger that sustained other serious injuries (they were 3 broken ribs & a collapsed lung).

There were 5 people in the vehicle that included the Driver, 3 out of 5 walked away without a scratched it was only the one other passenger along with Jamie that sustained serious injuries. Jamie received the worst out of the accident, by getting a head injury along with a broken left arm. Not too long after I spent time seeing my brother in the state he was in, Jane & I had to head back to Englehart because I had to get back to school.

Before summer of 2001 began I was able to make it through the 7th Grade Level, after a while I was also able to return to the Hospital to visit my brother again. During the time that I was away my brother had been moved from the 2nd Floor I.C.U to the 6th Floor, so instead of going to the 2nd Floor I went to the 6th Floor to see my brother.

There was a time that I will never forget, I, along with a few other people had went to lunch one day, the event itself took place when we got back up to the 6th Floor.

On the way to see Jamie my dad stopped to make a call except I should have told him to see Jamie 1st cause its important for him to see Jamie or vice versa. When we went in to see Jamie minus my dad, the way Jamie looked just broke my heart. I felt like crying again because Jamie was in a state of panic, his nurse had removed his breathing tube and he was very agitated because he looked like he couldn't breathe.

The nurse had put a mask on him but he wouldn't allow it to give him oxygen to breathe, so he was showing whomever that he couldn't breathe by looking like a fish that was struggling for air. His arms were also tied down to prevent him from hurting himself & others if he were to ever struggle for anything like air.

Jane had stood by his face and doing her best to calm him down, I was on the opposite side from Jane holding Jamie's hand to hopefully give him comfort . . .

No such luck.

Jane looked at me and said *"Go Annie, you don't need to see him like this"*, so I left on the edge of breaking down. Once I made it back out to the hallway I went to see what my dad was doing, I found him still on the phone talking.

I was able to get his attention with hand signals saying *"They took out his breathing tube, he isn't taking it very well"*, not long after my dad went in to see Jamie except it was after he was given something to put him to sleep. I felt so upset with my dad for being so careless, and not being there for his son when his son needed him most. A few days later Jane & I headed back to Englehart so that I could finish school. During the time I was away & graduating the seventh grade level I was able to talk to Jamie over the phone. Since he was never put back on the breathing tube his voice sounded a little harsher than normal (like having a sore throat), I asked *"Hey Jamie, how are you doing?"* he answered back the best he could saying *"I am okay"*, I then asked *"Are you feeling better??"* I could hear him softly say *"Yeah"* I then said *"I miss you, brother"* he replied saying *"I miss you too"*.

As I was nearing my years end of Elementary School life I was beginning to feel a little off health wise, it was during the time that I was doing alter serving; I felt like I was about to loose my stomach so I acted like I was about to be sick yet stayed calm, next I felt like my body was heating up like I was having a high fever. I never told Tracy about what happened since even though it was about my health, I stayed quiet thinking nothing else would happen later.

I didn't really think much of what was going on with myself because I still had my focus on upcoming School events like Graduation. I had absolutely no idea what kind of awards I would be receiving, besides attending school & participating in different sports. I don't remember how many awards I had received but I know that they dealt with

Basketball, Volleyball, Track & Field & Public Speaking along with my duty as Cross Bearer.

I was able to make it through the 8th Grade Level, I was able to graduate.

Sometime after the Ceremony, I joined my own private Entourage that included my mom who came for the special event, after I met up with everybody I began to feel really hot like my body temperature was beginning to boil over, so I tried to tell whoever that I had to get out of the Church because I was getting really hot to the point where I almost couldn't breathe. I was like "I need to get out of this place, I am feeling really hot" of course without waiting for a response I took off towards the door with my arms full, I could have taken a detour and used the side door to the Church but I was in such a rush I ran right past the door to the side entrance. Not knowing the result of what will happen once I made it outside of the church I kept running and was able to make it down all the front steps except the 2nd last, just my luck I ended up tripping and having worn 2 inch heels I'm surprised I didn't break either of my ankles but I did scrape my left knee really bad. I could feel myself flying in slow motion from the 2nd last step of the Church to the hard pavement and dropping all my awards in front of me and feeling sharp pain in my left knee the feeling almost made me pass out, what is a lot worse was that my entire class & their families were gathered by the road looking at me on the ground. The next thing I know I hear Tracey, Sandra & my mom coming to my aid after finding out that I had fell down (I had this urge to cry only I never did), I had never felt so awful & embarrassed before in my life especially in front of my entire class.

Once I was able to get my knee cleaned & bandaged up I attended the scheduled dance for grade eight graduation, once the feeling of joy & excitement of that event came & went I decided to visit my family down south for the summer; it was sometime during the summer that my mom noticed that I was limping because of me injuring my knee from grade eight grad, she asked me "Why are you limping Annie?" "my knee is still sore" I had replied, this was summer of 2001 that my mom began to worry & wonder why it was taking so long for a knee wound like I had to get better.

The average time for a wound like mine to heal should have been two weeks, except the pain I had lasted a lot longer. My mom brought her concern to Jane hoping that the pain I was going through would be dealt with, only it never was dealt with.

By the end of 2001 September I then got myself enrolled into Englehart High School (EHS)—the same High School my oldest brother Bob went to.

EHS, Friends & 1st Symptoms

The first day of High School Jane's daughter Teresa took me to Englehart High, to get me registered for my classes. I met my homeroom teacher, along with another student. The homeroom teachers name is Ms. Dorrell & the student's name is Annie Morrison, we went to the hall and picked our lockers. Since the lockers were numbered I picked #1 and my new friend picked locker #2 I figured that since my oldest brother went to the same place & made friends easily, I would be able to do the same as well.

Annie and I had the same physical education, TAG & homeroom teacher. We became best friends as soon as we met. We also found out that we were born on the same day, month & year, the only difference is that I was older than my friend in terms of time of our birth.

Annie was quite shy, quiet & laid back very different from myself, of course I was quite hyper, talkative &

outgoing. In other words Annie & I became inseparable, I would go over to her place to hang out, sleep over, do what normal teenager girls do: gossip, do homework & just enjoy each others company.

Btw this point in time the pain in my knee had begun to leave and I was feeling better, everything with me did seem to go back to normal having a new best friend & facing new challenges that usually comes with being in School.

After my first few months of doing schoolwork, dealing with bullying, harassment & just fitting in, I was able to meet my first guy friend. His name is Ryan Knight, Ryan & I met during Phys. Ed Class, we began seeing each other throughout High School.

We had an interesting relationship, nothing mushy or anything just interesting. Ryan seemed more into making sure that his school work was done, I of course did the same thing yet hoped that Ryan would have been more talkative with me along with spent more time with me.

The only time I would go to Ryan's house was if there was a certain special occasion going on, we never did anything alone. There was one event before things got confusing & very bad for my health was a High School Dance (Christmas Prom), it was fairly fancy.

I dressed in a nice, elegant black sparkly dress and two-inch black high-heeled shoes with a black scarf. Ryan was dressed like he was going to a ballgame or something he was dressed in beige pants and a cotton plaid shirt with semiworn running shoes, of course you could say I was dressed to impress since I was more of an outsider than anything else I actually didn't attract any attention.

During the dance I did my best to get Ryan to get his groove on to fast music, except he never budged from his seat. After the dance I went back to doing my best to get through my school work while dealing with people teasing me and talking behind my back.

During one of the school activities some things began to happen, it was badminton season at Englehart High. Annie & I were in Phys. Ed in the gym with our classmates, we were all practicing badminton. We were practicing for fun on my request, during one of the times where I had to serve on my side I swung my racket back, except before I could swing it forward I felt my right hand get tingly. I looked over at my hand and noticed that it was pale & going numb (like being out in the freezing cold for too long), I put my racket down and stared at my right hand until the feeling came back again. Once the feeling was back I looked over at my friend who was standing there patiently waiting for me to take my turn. I felt a little confused yet brushed it off, as if there was nothing wrong at all.

Hospital, Meds & Appearance

One day Jane & I received a phone call from my mom saying *"Annie you need to go see the doctor sometime soon"*, there was a firm tone in her voice and she said *"You need to get blood tests done"*. Even though there was little bit of urgency in her voice Jane & I didn't think it was anything serious, I said *"No, I feel fine, everything is ok"*.

So Jane & I blew off the warning that was given to us, after awhile I began to get more & more joint pains with numbness in my hands & feet.

Since it was the end of January there was still snow on the ground, the cold itself had begun to affect my physical health. My wrists & ankles would get sore, feel numb & turn ghostly white, and as each day went by the symptoms that I had been getting kept returning. There was a time where I had been shovelling snow with one of Jane's sons, he & I were at the end of the driveway.

I felt like I couldn't handle the cold anymore and I began to cry and said "*I want to go inside, I am really cold*", and he said "*No, you stay out here, you don't need to go inside*". Sometime later I let my tears fall for about 5 minutes then decided to leave going inside without telling him, I did my best to not look like I was upset when I really was.

Jane finally decided to take me to get my blood work done, when it came to needles kids would usually feel petrified with just a look but I looked like I could handle anything no matter how bad the situation. After the first few times there would be more & more each time we went back, sometime later I was told that I would be taken to a Hospital in Timmins, Ontario.

The last time I was in Timmins was in the previous year, Jane's daughter had opened a weight loss clinic there. I helped with painting & redecorating the place since it was for business, not fun & games, the place had high walls with a little kitchen in the back along with a room that was transformed into a spare bedroom the entire place looked huge.

I never thought that I would have had to go to a Hospital in the same area the following year for my health, of course it had to be done so Jane & I went in to Timmins District to get me registered for a Hospital card. Then we were taken upstairs to one of the rooms where I was to stay that night, I never imagined staying I just figured it was a visit not an overnight stay.

We were brought to a room with 2 beds, it may have been semi-private since there was only 1 person (myself) staying there was one bed already made up for me. I had no clue what was going on I just went along with whatever I was told to do, the only other time I was in the hospital had been to visit my brother. But for me to stay in a Hospital it seemed a little scary.

The bed that was made up for me was across from the bathroom then once I got situated I was granted to do whatever I wanted except leave the floor I was on, I was allowed to walk around, which was interesting, I was also granted to entertain myself with a provided Television, VCR, along with video games that were available to any child that stayed there, I even hung out with the nurses at the nurses station.

I was permitted to call my family with the phone that had been provided in the room I was staying in, I even called Jane & her family and talked to them all as well. I managed to speak to everybody with a brave voice without crying, I truly never thought I would be in a place where people are sick to get better.

I was able to act brave like the big girl that I was, being almost 16 I had to stay strong and not let anything bother me even though I was bullied in High School. I had a feeling that I was the only one in that hospital floor, because I did not see anyone else but myself along with the nurses.

As the day faded into night I began to feel very isolated for the first time in my life, before falling asleep I lay there finally realising that I may have to be in this place where people get special care for awhile I just didn't know for how long. My emotions began to catch up to me though, I soon began to toss & turn in my bed hoping that the night would pass soon.

I chose to lay facing the window in the room looking out at the dark sky of the night, the feeling of sadness began to build from the pit of my stomach and crawled up to my chest & throat.

At that moment I began to think:

'What is my family thinking right now?'

'What are they feeling when I am here in the hospital like this for the first time in my life?'

'How long or how often do I have to be in a hospital like this?'

'Will I be in a hospital for more or less than a day?'

'Will I be in a hospital for more or less than a week?'

'Will I be in a hospital for more or less than a month?'

'Will I be in a hospital for more or less than a year?'

All these questions were running around in my mind for the first time in my life, I then began thinking of my family and the tears that I held in began to build up from the sad feeling inside had started to fall.

I ended up crying myself to sleep in hopes that I would be able to go home tomorrow.

The next morning Jane & Teresa came to see me bringing along my suitcase full of my clothes, cause all I had were the clothes from the day before. I had washed up before they arrived so all I had to do was pick out what I wanted to wear for the day, once I was dressed I was told that I would be taken by plane to another Hospital only this one would be in Toronto, Ontario.

We all soon met the EMT's they had a stretcher with them for me to lay on, I put my shoes & jacket on then went over and checked out the stretcher.

I was then advised to climb onto it and get comfortable, I was then strapped down like I were an actual patient.

We were lead to the little Aircraft Carrier that would take us to the Hospital in Toronto, once we got situated we did our best to get as comfortable as we could.

The ride was quite long and tiring, I had slept most of the way, once we arrived we were taken to a private room since it was just myself & Jane.

I guessed that most Hospital rooms were bland since there were no colors of any kind in the room, the only thing on the walls was one single landscape picture hanging on the right side of the Hospital bed. Jane & I got settled in and soon met a nurse that would be tending to me while I was there, it wasn't long before I began to notice lots of medications being brought into the room every time my nurse came to see me.

Not long after the medication had begun to arrive, I was then given an IV Line which was put into my hand.

The amount of medication went from five to ten, I noticed at times the medications were the same medications or multiple of one with a single of another medication. The number of medications kept on getting larger and larger as the days went by, I had absolutely no idea what was going on all I did was do what I was told without asking any questions.

There was one particular medication that I had begun to really hate, it was a chalky medication called *"Kayexalate"* it had 2 different parts that were combined together. A powder and some kind of syrup that would be mixed together in a Styrofoam cup, when I smelt it the only thing that came to mind was *"cement"*.

After I smelt the medication I could already feel my stomach begin to churn like I was going to vomit everything I ate that day, I made a disgusted face like *'Yuck'* yet did my best to keep my stomach steady. Once I took a mouthful I literally felt like vomiting whatever in my stomach, since this was just the beginning I still looked normally slim with nothing wrong . . .

Until after about two weeks of taking in daily medication . . .

Once I took a mouth full I spit it out right away into a plastic kidney shaped dish, my nurse then said *"If you do that with the rest of it, I will just get you more so you better take it now & get it over with"*. I hated it yet did as I was told, I kept taking huge mouth full of the medication from the Styrofoam cup.

Both Jane & the nurse began coaxing me by saying *"Swallow it, just swallow it don't think about it just gulp it down"*, I did the best I could taking the medication without throwing up I did it until there was no more left. The Kayexalate is a powder except if it sits to long it turns into a solid like "cement", so if I didn't drink it, it would be a lot worse than having it as a liquid.

That night I did my best to sleep after dealing with whatever other medication that was brought in for me to take, not long after I fell asleep I soon began to feel tremendous pain in my abdomen which resulted in me having to toss and turn in the Hospital bed. The pain got to a point where my stomach felt so awful, it woke me up and was not able to get comfortable, so I woke Jane up who was sleeping on the cot beside my bed I let her know I was in pain.

I reached out to her and said "*I need to go to the washroom*" Jane got up and helped me to the bathroom. I leaned over the toilet and figured the pain I had was from nausea, minutes later I felt something coming out in the opposite end so I turned around and soon the pain soon began to disappear.

My nights followed the same routine as the first, being in the washroom.

Soon I began to feel really heavy I looked at my reflection in the bathroom mirror one day after brushing my teeth, I couldn't even recognize myself anymore. My cheeks were chunkier like a chipmunk's, instead of wearing pyjama bottoms, I wore a night gown that a senior would wear while being in a retirement home.

I began to really notice that my body had begun to look a lot bigger than it usually would, my hands were fat on top and my stomach began to bulge out like I was pregnant I even began having trouble getting in and out of bed. I soon began to really feel ugly with myself I didn't have time to think of what would happen next, my weight had went from a regular 100 pounds up to 167 pounds.

I would always get my weight checked every morning while in the Hospital, sometimes while I was there my mom came to see how I was doing. I had never seen my mom look scared before since she could barely recognize her own daughter looking this way, my entire body was bulging from the waist down including my arms & hands.

I actually felt as ugly as I looked in terms of my weight I had to sit on a scale to get it checked instead of standing up, my weight was so bad that I wasn't able to stand on my own feet for longer than 5 minutes at a time. When it came to food on my tray it was like I couldn't even look at it like I used to, one day I had got one of my favourite pasta dishes: lasagne. I uncovered the lasagne on my tray one evening only instead of digging into it I just stared at it, the smell of melted cheese covered in tomato sauce & pasta all layered together looked so tempting yet I couldn't bear to touch it.

I knew that if I ate it the medication that I was to take later on would make me just bring it right back up again, the only thing I saw that I knew my stomach could handle was a small package of Cracker Barrel block cheese that was also provided on my tray.

Everything else I chose not to touch that was included with the lasagne.

The kayexalate was the only reason I had rejected food in general because I knew that every time I took it everything in my stomach would come right back up again, at one point I decided on improvising on taking the *"Kayexalate"* I had asked Jane to get me one of those cups of apple sauce. So she retrieved the apple sauce and brought it to me, I put the Kayexalate medication in the apple sauce.

I then proceeded in taking the medication that way, figured maybe it would not be half as bad as taking it from a Styrofoam cup.

Before this entire ordeal began I had the ability to lean down & touch my toes, I would be able to sit on a bed (I would be able to sit crossed legged lean forward and put my head on the floor or bed in front of me). At the present time with the weight I had gained I couldn't do that anymore I would feel pain in my lower back like an actual senior as well, the medications that I took went from five to ten all the way up to twenty-two different medications. The Kayexalate was one of the many medications that I had to take.

The weight that I had gained wasn't even due to muscle it was more fluid because I could do an imprint of my finger in my skin, press down and the skin wouldn't jump back it would be lower than the rest of the body. If I were to ever sit down on the floor I wouldn't be able to get back up on my own I would need help to stand up, I had never felt so disgusted in myself before in my life.

Warning, Suicide & Coma

One evening my mom and her boyfriend came to visit while I was hanging around in an area down the hall from my room, there were lounge chairs in a semi-circle Jane & I were enjoying each other's company when I saw my mom I felt good to see her.

My mom sat in a lounge chair across from Jane & I, while my mom's boyfriend stood just behind the one my mom was sitting in.

My mom then said *"We need to talk"* I looked at my mom expectantly and asked *"What about?"* my mom replied *"We know you that you need to be taken care of, you need to come home with mom"*, I looked over at Jane with an expression that said *"Please help me"* Jane then said *"Its up to you Annie, what do you want to do?"* then my mom said *"If you stay with Jane you are to do exactly what she says, if you want to get better you are to take your medication, because if you don't you will die in two weeks"*.

When I heard my mom say *'die in two weeks'* I stood up with the help from Jane taking her hand and left my mom and her boyfriend in the lounge area, I left with Jane feeling a sense of anger and sadness boiling up inside me as I headed to my room with Jane right behind me.

As Jane & I were walking heading back to my hospital room she had said to me *"Your mom is cursing your life, that's just not right; I'll take you home, everything will be alright"* I actually wanted to cry only chose to hold back the tears, since I had gained so much weight I wasn't able to walk very far like I usually did before this whole ordeal began, I couldn't walk far without nearly collapsing or gasping for breath anymore.

I was a very athletic girl that all I wanted to do was get good grades, and make it through to be someone special like a registered nurse. A few days later Jane & I were sent back to Englehart by train because I had to go back to school, also the fact that since I had gained so much weight I wasn't able to fit in any of my own clothes anymore. I wore the same kind of clothes Jane would wear only in my own style.

Jane was a widowed mother that lived in a 2 bedroom bungalow with a finished basement, she had 4 kids that had already grown up & had their own family's. I wore baggy jeans, white t-shirt, a grey cotton sweater & black running shoes with no backs almost like slippers all large, I also had to wear special white leggings to keep the circulation going. I had to have help getting from place to place because of my weight gain, I felt a lot worse going to school looking the way I did.

Before my illness I looked very tiny like a normal teenager but because of my weight gain I looked more like an elephant, I went to school for as many days as I could handle until I couldn't get out of bed.

All this took a span of less than a week it wasn't long before I began to get stubborn and refused to take my medication, I may have enjoyed the pampering treatment but what I hated the most was the time I had to take my medication which was three times a day.

Everything that was happening to me got to a point where I actually became delusional like talking to myself, I just did not act like I usually did I even began asking questions about everything that was happening to me like questioning why I was taking medication in general. Soon Jane began saying *"If you want to get better you need to exercise"* so I started doing laps inside around the house, Jane began to join me in doing the laps.

I did as many laps as I could until I wasn't able to stand anymore. My previous symptoms of numbness & joint pains in my arms and legs soon returned.

I was still advised to take the Kayexalate at night before dinner, then sometime while watching TV or end of a movie, that I would vomit everything that I had eaten for dinner. Every evening would be the same take the medication eat food then everything I ate would be all over the front of my clothes. It was a never ending ritual that got to a point where I couldn't take it anymore, everything that I was going through became way to much for me.

Everything about my situation put me in a position where I couldn't even leave Jane's house anymore, my health got so bad to the point where I couldn't even leave my bed. I soon began to devise a plan, that when Jane was not around that I would commit suicide.

Plan A: Use arm of glasses to stab into chest

Plan B: Use a sharp knife from the kitchen to stab into chest

One late afternoon Jane let me know that she would be having a shower not long after I felt a surge of adrenaline to execute my plan, when I knew that Jane was out of sight I took my glasses and broke the arm using the steel end and pushed it into my chest only my hands became really sweaty, and slippery.

When I realised it wasn't working I got out of bed and ran to the kitchen, going straight to the drawer where the knives were and pushed it into my chest, I had underestimated how much weight I had gained because when I ran it was like a herd of raging elephants.

I knew that my suicide attempt could have been successful if Jane didn't stop me, I knew that if Plan A didn't work that Plan B most definitely would have.

Not long after my failed suicide attempts, I was taken to get my glasses fixed, after my failed suicide attempts I still had to take the medication and the Kayaxalate until I was at the point of delirium.

I began to say things that didn't sound like they made sense like gibberish. I was just not acting like I usually did, my health got worse and worse. Not long after seeing how bad I was Jane received a phone call from a Doctor that was in Toronto. They advised Jane to get me an emergency flight to Toronto.

I had had a seizure on the flight to the Hospital. During the seizure I could see myself bothering the medic like messing around with his facial hair and stethoscope, sometime later I was out cold. Once I was at the Hospital

I had had another seizure. I could see my mom & dad standing beside stretcher that I was laying on.

When she arrived at the Hospital she heard her mom ask the medic "what's wrong with my daughter?" I noticed that my mom had a worried tone in her voice, my dad with my mom also asked wondering, what was wrong with me and why I was so sick because of the way I looked.

I assumed that I looked really horrible since I could see myself in nothing but a green nightgown. The medic had to check if my eyes were responsive by putting liquid in my eyes. I was aware of my surroundings, but I could not speak I just was not able to communicate or move or do anything, probably cause of the fact that I had another seizure.

I began to see things as if I were in a dream, having no idea what was going on until I began to see medical staff spinning toward me like a strange video game. The scariest thing was that the top half of a doctor would spin toward me and stop 2 inches from my face, I wanted to scream in fear except I wasn't able to do so.

Coma, Dialysis & Waking Up

I was soon moved to a bed in the Intensive Care Unit in Saint Michael's Hospital. It was during that time that I had another seizure that left me in a comatose state. Also while I was in a coma, the only people that were allowed to stay with me was my family.

During the time that I was in the coma I was sent up to one of the higher floors, I had had another round of seizures, I had to be sent back down to the Intensive Care Unit. This time I had to have a breathing tube put in, because after the last seizure my lungs had bled.

My mom soon found out that my kidney's were shutting down. Whatever I had was attacking my kidneys. My Doctor told my mom that I might not make it through the night. My dad had actually stated *"We should arrange for her funeral."* My mom argued back saying *"No! I will not arrange for my daughter's funeral she is only 16! For Christ sake, she has her whole life ahead of her. You must put her on dialysis*". The Doctor went on about getting a priest for the last rights saying "No. Arrange the funeral there is nothing we can do." My mom had had enough and felt a surge of anger build up inside, my mom went up to the dialysis unit and requested them to put me on the list to have my kidney's filtered.

Once that was done my mom went back down to be with me.

In my state of mind I was able to open my eyes and move my head around. I was able to see things that did not look right to me. I noticed that I was laying down and seeing people at the foot of my bed, I felt lost in place where I could not move or speak. I felt very frightened.

I was able to see my brother's come & see me, when the time came for me to have dialysis I began to feel a lot better the stuff I was seeing soon went away. I still had a breathing tube so I couldn't talk, I saw my oldest brother Bob leaning against the bed and he was crying I had never seen him cry before.

I saw that Jamie had his Portable CD Player with him, he placed the headphones on me and I began to bounce my head around like I was rocking to the beat of the music. I turned and saw my dad he was wearing his orange monk robes, I felt a little upset towards him because of what he did to me when I was younger.

I even noticed Tom during this time while he was dating my mother, between the time I saw my family I began to feel wet under my body. I reached down and found out that I was soaked. My body was beginning to let go of the fluid that was trapped between my bone & skin. The bed pad under my body was soaked and needed to be changed often.

Once the fluid was completely gone all there was left of me was skin & bone, I looked so small in my bed under the white hospital blanket. A few days later I was able to get my breathing tube taken out since my lungs had healed, although my throat was raw I was able to write down what I wanted.

The first thing I wrote down was "*I am hungry*". Well being in the hospital with so many things going on around me along with me not be aware of people walking by my bed there was nothing going into my stomach. The next thing I noticed was my dad by my side in regular clothes, noticed him gather me up and take me out where he had parked the family van.

I noticed him driving to the end of the earth, the next thing I felt was the back of the van tipping up all the while hearing voices.

The voices were calling out my name saying . . .

"*Annie . . .*"

"*Annie . . .*"

"*Annie . . .*"

"*Annie . . .*"

"*ANNIE!!!*"

"*ANNIE!!!!*"

The last voice I heard was Jamie, I was able to hear him loud & clear. Feeling around in my mouth and noticing that I didn't have a breathing tube in, I had the urge to cry & it was fierce.

The next thing I was doing was calling out . . .

"*MOM!!!!*"

"*MOM!!!!*"

I did not stop calling out until I saw someone appear in my line of sight, it was a nurse that said "*What's the matter honey?*" in a caring tone. The only thing I said to the nurse was "*I want my mom*", I then began to cry and couldn't stop. I heard my mom come saying "*Hey baby. Everything will be ok.*" I asked "*Can you ask Jane if I can come home with you?*" I began to calm down some when my mom said "*Yes, I will take care of it.*" My mom had to argue a little bit with Jane to allow my mom to take me home, finally I was able to stay with my mom.

Once I was stable enough to leave the Intensive Care Unit I was sent back up to the room on the higher floor. I was able to see not just my parents but also my brothers as well. When I got to my room I noticed a lot of get well cards, flowers along with a signed bed sheet from my High School friends.

The bed sheet had the words "*Get Well Annie*" on it with signatures of most of the students I had gone to School with up in Englehart, the sheet was pinned up on the wall facing the hospital bed. My visitors were not only my family and their friends, there were Jane and her family as well.

There was just one problem it was that every time Jane and her family were with me, my mom would be resting only when my mom returned I would be very disoriented and confused after Jane and her family left. It wasn't long before my mom realised that I would always get confused and disoriented from only Jane's visits, my mom chose to prohibit visits from Jane and her family.

Once that was done I would be fine, nothing wrong at all.

My mom even advised the nurses at the desk to filter all the phone calls that went to my room, my mom said "*If there are any calls coming from Jane or any of her kids, please do not allow it to go through*" they granted the request by saying "*Yes, we will make sure the calls are filtered Mrs. Kittiphanh*".

Once that was done the only phone calls I received were my own family.

BSB, 1ˢᵗ Trip Home & Sick Kids

When I found out that Jane was not happy about the orders that my mom had given the nurse, I began to wonder *'Why is Jane not allowed to speak with me?'* since I had only spoken to Jane once. My mom then explained to me that during my last phone conversation I had with Jane, it wasn't 5 minutes before I turned ghostly white and vomited.

It was after that conversation that my mom got really fed up and said "No more phone calls from Jane!!" my mom was able to calm me down and later I began to listen to my music, the Backstreet Boys. Their newest album released that same year was *The Hits: Chapter One* CD that I had received when I was first admitted to the Hospital there in Toronto, the CD was in my Portable CD Player.

I was able to recall my dad forwarding the CD to the very last song entitled *"Drowning"*, when I had a good day I would sing along with another song which was *"I Want It*

That Way" I would sing like no one was watching. On one of my good days I was singing along to "*Drowning*" my nurse had commented saying "*She could be a singer one day*", I kept singing along with my Backstreet Boys in my ears.

After about 2 weeks of being in the Hospital I was able to go home, my mom was able to arrange my first limo trip to pick us up. There was also a fruit basket since the ride was long, I was advised to rest but I sat up wanting to see everything.

Since it was my first time in a limo I soaked up the entire experience all the way home, I felt like a famous star, I always had a smile on my face. When my mom & I got to the house there was a sign on the garage door that read "*Welcome Home Annie*" in big letters made out of thin coloured paper, the whole thing brought me to tears because it looked so awesome.

When the limo door opened I looked out and there stood my brother Jamie, as I climbed out of the limo I wrapped my arms around Jamie I had missed him so much. Once I stepped inside I felt like it was my first time in the house that my family was in, I remembered the last time I was there my mom was having a glamour session going on.

It was a few months before my health went downhill.

I went into my mom's office where all of my belongings were which was all my clothes from Jane's house. I sorted through all my clothes to see what I had. Once that was done I was taken upstairs to my bedroom. I looked around and admired how my mom had decorated it with a homemade canopy above my bed.

It was made of different shades of purple and I felt in awe of the whole thing. I then went through my other stuff that was around the room. I soon settled in and I soaked up being home as much as I could. One day I had spent 15 minutes sitting just outside of the patio door. The back was fenced in and there wasn't much to the backyard except a tool shed that my moms boyfriend had built along with a hot tub for my brother to use for therapy.

One day I saw my mom sitting out on the back step; my mom's boyfriend was the first person to notice me which made my mom to turn and look since she was sitting on the step.

My mom asked "*Would you like to come outside?*" "*Yes, please*" I had replied, so my mom moved out of the way and helped me step outside.

Since I was still weak I needed help with a lot of things like sitting down and standing up, it wasn't long before I began to get tired. My mom noticed right away and brought me back into the house, my mom sat me down on the couch that was in the room beside the dining area.

My mom soon noticed that I looked really pale, she looked to see what was wrong, then called 911. I was sent to the Emergency room in an ambulance. After awhile I felt fine, it wasn't long before my mom realised that I was allergic to the sun because when she saw me not moving or breathing it scared her.

Inside the house, I felt like I had tunnel vision I couldn't see anything in the corners of my eyes I also felt heavy in my chest and I had this urge of wanting to cry but couldn't. I ended up in the Emergency room three times in that one month, each time going in an ambulance. My body was acting up so much that I had to be taken back to the Hospital in Toronto I stayed there for another few months.

During my stay there my oldest brother Bob would visit so I asked him to bring his laptop with him, so I could play games on it when I felt bored. Ever since I was brought to the Hospital, I would stay up half the night crying because I missed my mom so much.

My health got so bad to a point where I was having a hard time eating and keeping food down, my mom chose to have a GJ-Tube put in. My mom & I began arguing back and forth that I was able to eat without the tube, I kept saying "*I can do this, I can prove to you that I can eat and keep my food down*", In truth even though I said this my stomach would always act up at the mere sight of not just hospital food but regular food of any kind.

I realised that besides the fact of wanting to forget everything I was going through without help I eventually gave up and said "*I agree to have a gastric tube put in, to have a GJ-tube*". Once the procedure was done to have the GJ-Tube put in I saw it and the next thing I thought was '*What the heck is this in my stomach*', the situation got to a point where I would ask "*What is this, can I remove this?*" '*motioning to the GJ-Tube*' I soon began to panic and said "*No I need that*" I guessed that I did need it the tube in after all.

The purpose of the GJ-Tube was to help with my nutrition whatever I needed to ingest would be put into the GJ-Tube so that it would bypass my mouth, I wouldn't have to worry about putting anything in my mouth. Sometime later I found out that my Doctor's of Saint Michael's Hospital decided to clean their hands of me and send me to The Hospital For Sick Children. I supposed to go to that hospital before, except there was a virus outbreak. Since my immune system was low from chemotherapy, there was no way I was going to end up better than I already was.

Before I left Saint Michael's Hospital the Asian Doctor that I met during my stay came to see how I was doing, I felt happy to see him cause once I was transferred I wouldn't see him again.

I was then taken to Sickkids, I was transported in an ambulance. I began to really like the Hospital. Cause soon as I had arrived, there was color!! Not just plain white, when I was in my first room my health still acted up, I had no idea if it was the kind or type of room or the atmosphere or what it was, all I knew was that I had seizures and other things come back. By this point I had begun to develop the raccoon rash or the butterfly effect rash it was called. I Found out that many lupus patients like myself would develop the rash which showed on parts of the body I wasn't sure what was worse looking like a fat chipmunk or having a rash that made me look really contagious.

It wasn't long before I was moved from one room to another, the number on my room was #50 the other room I was switched to was #9.

I had spent five months in Sickkids and went through a lot and am very grateful to all the nurses & doctors that had taken care of me, there are no words to describe how appreciative I am of certain nurses & doctors that were in charge of my case when I was a patient there. There was a time where I could have been on with my mother while at Sickkids only I ended up going home instead, it was during Halloween my mom & I had signed a paper stating that I had agreed to appear on TV.

During my stay at Sickkids there was one particular Doctor that I began to really like, whenever my Doctor came to see me I would always ask about this one other particular Doctor; he had a lazy eye and I really liked him. There was a male nurse that I had taken care of me once and I thought he was a pretty cool guy, he told me his story of having surgery in the same Hospital; he then became a nurse in the same place, there were a few other nurses that I believe were really awesome.

Christmas, Make-A-Wish & Rehab

The new room number was 9 I was told that once I had switched rooms, I didn't have as many episodes with my health as I did before. I still had symptoms but they didn't show up as often as they usually did. After I was moved I began to feel a lot better each day. I still would have my bad days. The one and only thing that did not improve was my nutrition.

I had my 24 hour feeding every night so I didn't have much to eat each during the day, and my 24 hour feeding through the night would replace what was or would be missing. I always had a hard time keeping my food down I would try but food in general just would not be as appetizing as it usually would. There was also the fact of my weight that was another issue in itself my body still rejected food and I didn't eat as much as I was supposed to.

Sometime before thanksgiving my mom & her boyfriend came to visit me, during the visit my mom went out to do something so it was just myself & my mom's boyfriend in my hospital room. At some point while I was watching TV I looked over at the boyfriend who was sitting near by the window looking at a flyer, he looked up at me and I out of the blue asked him "When are going to marry my mother?" I could tell from the look on his face that he was in shock that I actually asked the question; I wasn't sure what happened after that all I knew was that I was able to go home for half a day for the Ceremony & be my mom's flower girl, I found out later that everything dealing with preparation of the Ceremony was throughout the time span of three days from the Priest, Catering, the dress & the flowers. Once everything with the Ceremony was done I was taken back to the Hospital, my mom made sure to develop the photos from the Ceremony.

A few months later it was Christmas. I was feeling very down because I had begun to feel ill, I was ill to the point where I had to be in isolation so I wasn't allowed to leave my room all Christmas Day. So for me to be or feel happy was a little difficult for the Holiday. It wasn't until sometime around dinner on Christmas Day that I had guests.

As soon as I saw who my guests were I felt a lot better. My guests were my entire family, they had brought Christmas to me. When I saw the gifts my family brought I thought 'Hmm, maybe Christmas wouldn't be so bad after all'. I was all smiles and close to tears because my family came to see me, I went from not being able to leave my room or do anything then: *KABOOM!!* Family.

One of my gifts that made me scream in excitement was from one of my nurses, the gift had made me scream because once I made the first tear in the wrapping paper I saw my favourite music group. I had received a board game it was the Backstreet Boys Around The World Game it was based on their *Black & Blue Album*/Tour. I had never felt so well & happy until that moment I was '*So shocked*' because I had received something that had the Backstreet Boys on it. Once all the presents were opened and the stockings were looked through, my brothers & I chilled out for a little bit as well as posed for photos that were taken and developed that same night.

I may have been in bed for the entire holiday; however the Christmas event in my room was able to make me feel so much better **smiles wide**. About a month later I began to feel really sick. During one of my visits with my mom, I wasn't able to stay awake. My mom knew something was wrong since I wasn't able to stay awake long enough to spend time with her. My mom advised me to sleep and right after I was out like a light, my mom found out that if I didn't get through this next flu I wouldn't make it so my mom had to make a quick decision she didn't want to lose her only daughter.

While I was sleeping I received an unexpected visitor that I didn't know. The nurse explained to me that the lady was someone from the Make-A-Wish Foundation. Their goal/mission was to ask those that were ill to make 3 wishes, almost like Cinderella. They said that I was allowed to ask for 3 wishes. I nodded in understanding and said "My first would be to see and meet Nick Carter of the Backstreet Boys". They said that it could be arranged. The other 2 wishes were to see my dad (who was in California at that time) and to visit my grandmother over in Laos.

Once my wishes were made I went back to sleep. A few days later I received 2 visitors that I did not recognize, they explained to me that they were from the Make-A-Wish Foundation. They would be with me through making one of my wishes come true. I soon found out that it would be my first wish to be granted, to see and meet Nick Carter of the Backstreet Boys. Every time they came to see me they would bring updates of what I would be doing when it came to my first wish.

When it came to the godmother's visits I would forget what they do, since when I made my wish I didn't think it would happen. I am very thankful to have met the lady's from the Make-A-Wish Foundation for everything they have done to make mine & other children's life better by granting wish's and by giving them hope & making their life better, along with make a child's dream come true just like mine.

During one of my visits with the godmother's, they explained that I would be able to spend 5 minutes with Nick Carter himself before his solo concert. Once I heard that I felt a huge surge of excitement run through my body it was the second time I had felt so happy that I couldn't wait to see him (Nick Carter).

After a few more days I got a visit from a lady that specializes in which Rehab would be suitable for me, I told them that I would make things easy for them by saying that I would like to go to the same Rehab my older brother went to after his accident. The Rehab he went to (then) was Bloorview Macmillan Rehabilitation Centre (presently called Holland Bloorview Kids Rehabilitation Hospital), so once I explained my reason for choosing that Rehab everything was settled and days later I was discharged from the Hospital For Sick Children.

Rehab, Pampering
& Nick Carter

The day that I was to go to Rehab Centre I felt really excited because I was finally getting out of the Hospital. When my mom & I got there the nurses were wondering why my mom was back because before it was my brother that had the car accident went to the same place.

My mom explained *"Its Jamie's sister's turn to go to rehab"*. I was settled in a room only it was for a short time cause I was moved to another room, and I guess that whoever has the bed by the window owns the room.

That person gets different room mates, depending on if there are any rooms or beds available. I remember having 3 or 4 room mates, and sometimes I would have the room to myself. I also had visits from my family with my godmother's (Kelly & Michelle) from the Make-A-Wish Foundation.

One day I had a visit from my oldest brother Bob and stepdad, Tom. I looked at them and asked *"Hey guys."* I asked *"What's up??"* because they were in casual clothes, ready to have fun. Bob smiled and said *"Do you remember the wish you made to see and meet Nick Carter of the Backstreet Boys??"*. I looked at them in complete shock. Then, I thought back to the unexpected visitor I received back at Sick Kids, I looked down at myself and said *"I am so not dressed for the occasion."*

I heard both my oldest brother and stepdad laugh at my statement, since I was dressed all in black. Then I heard my stepdad say "Don't worry about it, you're going shopping". I looked up and smiled saying *"All right! Let me get my shoes on"* I grabbed my purple running shoes (my favourite color) and my black-and-yellow reversible jacket, and within two minutes I stood at the front door of the Rehab Centre.

Earlier, when I had noticed the stretch limo pull into the parking lot, I wondered who would be here in a stretch limo, but the thought never clicked until I saw Bob and Tom. That's when I realised it was for me. We were taken to a place where I would get a massage. I felt relaxed yet excited at the same time. My massage felt so good that I almost fell asleep. I wiggled every so often because the girl that was doing the massage would pass over my ticklish spots. Once the massage was done, I received a manicure at the same place. I of course chose purple nail polish. I was supposed to get a pedicure as well, only the time had run out. I didn't complain though since the massage and manicure had been fun and exciting in itself.

After showing off my nails we all went to a shopping mall where I could look around. My godmother's took me to the GAP store to pick out clothes, including an outfit to wear at the show. I was then taken to a restaurant where I would have dinner with my brother, stepdad and godmother's. The whole experience was captured by my godmother's taking picture after picture of me with my brother and stepdad.

Since I didn't have much energy to walk long distances, I was in a wheelchair most of the time I felt like a spoiled royal princess but I didn't mind. When dinner was done, we were taken to a venue where the show was held. We had to wait in the limo for a bit before being let in. I was then taken inside by wheelchair. I had passed by the merchandise table to see what they were selling. I chose a large t-shirt, a long sleeved shirt along with a poster which all had Nick Carter on all 3 items. I felt so overwhelmed being there that I couldn't say anything at all. I was speechless.

We were soon taken to an area where we had to sit and wait a little bit before seeing Nick Carter. We sat on comfortable couches, but when it was time for me to see Nick I had never felt so excited in so long. I was led down a hall and into a room. There on the right, leaning, against a counter talking to the host of MTV, was Nick Carter. He wore baggy jeans and a green t-shirt, when I walked into the room and heard his voice it sounded so familiar to me that it made me feel like me was 11 years old again.

There he was in person, looking as good as in videos, only better.

I was led to a part of the room where I could sit down and once I sat down I felt like jumping out of my skin. But I didn't, I kept my eyes on Nick Carter the entire time. Once Nick finished his interview with the host of MTV, one of my godmother's got his attention. They said *"Excuse me, Nick Carter I would like you to meet the Make-A-Wish Child"*. When she pointed at me, he looked me right in my eyes, then came down the steps, leaned down toward me and said *"Hey sweetie, can I have a hug?"* I nodded saying *'yes'* I felt so star struck that I couldn't say anything at all, I felt overwhelmed seeing *the* Nick Carter in person.

After I gave Nick a hug he said *"I'll sit down beside you"* he did, so close that our legs were touching. I had some things to ask or say to him, but I had forgotten how to use my voice. When he said *"Do you have any questions you would like to ask?"* I looked up at him and said the only thing that came to mind which was *"How could you be so cute?"* he looked up and said *"Hmm . . . I am not quite sure how to answer that question!"* and chuckled. When I was finally able to speak after that first question I then asked, *"What is going on with the guys and the group?"* *"Not much, they are on hiatus right now, you know, just taking a break"*, he asked *"Is there anything you would like me to autograph"* *"Yea, a page from your solo CD"*, I said looking for the case. He said *"Sure"* I grabbed the CD case that was in my lap and opened it up, I looked through the little booklet, *"Which section would you like me to autograph?"* he asked and I turned to the first page and picked the page where he had a 'Yea, I'm hot' posture on it. He was wearing a white t-shirt in the photo.

He was given a marker but when he tried to write with it, it didn't work *"Uh oh,"* he said *"marker problems"* The way he sounded when he said that made me giggle.

When he found a marker that did work he leaned toward me and asked *"What's your name?"* *"Anne-Marie"*

"*Ok, can you spell that for me?*" I was able to spell my name for him so that he could write it on the page I chose. He had written

"*To Anne-Marie Love Always Nick, Thanks For Coming*".

After he handed the booklet to one of the godmother's, he looked down at me and asked "*So are you going to be here for the show?*" in a sweet quiet voice. I looked down with a smile feeling my face get warm then leaned in and wrapped my arms around him.

He chuckled and wrapped his arms around me then offered a hand shake to Bob who was sitting on my other side, Nick offers his hand and says "*Hi I'm Nick Carter*" Bob shook his hand and said "*Bob, her oldest brother*", Tom stood up and offered his hand saying "*I'm Tom, her stepfather*" It was soon time to head out to find seats, but before we left Nick stood up and said "*It was nice to meet you,*" I looked up at him and said "*I read you are 6 feet tall, let's see the difference between you and me*" after I had help standing up I looked up at Nick and said "*Whoa . . . You are tall*" he looked at me with a chuckle and said "*Yes . . . Indeed I am*".

I stepped up to him putting my arms up and asked "*One more hug before I go?*" "Sure" he said before leaning down for me to put my arms around his neck, Nick & I were in an embrace for 2 minutes then when he was about to let go I pulled him forward to give him a kiss he moved his head for the kiss to land at the corner of his lips he seemed shocked yet smiled at the kiss. As I was walking away I quickly turned and said "*Thank you!!*"

I had my eyes on Nick the whole time then was lead back out through the hallway from where I once came, I noticed the line up of girls waiting to see Nick Carter.

As I passed the line up of girls the ones in front asked *"What is Nick like?" "Very sweet, kind, funny & caring"* was all I could say to them. When we all got back to the area where the stage was I realised that I had forgotten to get my poster signed.

I went to Michelle and asked *"Can you get Nick to sign this for me?"* "No problem" she said taking the poster back to Nick for him to autograph. We went to look for a place to sit and saw that the place was half packed already.

We looked for a spot beside the stage where the sound check table was, and I saw the equipment boxes with the name *"Carter"* on the side. I thought *'Hmm . . . I can sit on one of the boxes'* I turned to Kelly and asked *"Can I sit on one of the boxes?"* Kelly turned and said *"Yea, here is a cushion"*. My brother helped me onto the box then sat on the cushion on the box, my brother grabbed my belt loop for support in case I tipped over.

For me to be sitting beside the stage was like being VIP I felt so hyped I then saw other Nick Carter fans, I looked at them because I wasn't sure if they were allowed yet I looked at them and smiled *'sweetly'* even though I thought *'Hey, you're not allowed in this area'*. A few minutes later the girls that had joined me began to whisper and frantically wave like crazy, I then looked over to see Nick at the entrance from the backstage area.

My face went from a frown because of the girls to a huge smile because of seeing Nick, I felt warm inside, like I did when I first heard Nick's voice back in 1997.

I remembered during the show there was a song which Nick sang and he pointed at me.

When I saw that he pointed at me I clasped my hands together, close to my heart.

After the show finished we were all taken back to the Rehab Centre, I hadn't returned until midnight but I didn't mind being late. I had a great time seeing and meeting Nick Carter of the Backstreet Boys I had a blast at the show, a few days or so later that special meet with Nick Carter and the show I received my last visit from my godmother's since their job was done.

The godmother's had come by to give me the photos of my special moments with Nick Carter n' show every moment during that special day was captured.

A couple of weeks after that special event I had chemotherapy. I had to be sent to Sick Kids Hospital for the treatment, and since it was during the weekend, I was gone for 3 days.

Once my chemotherapy was done I was supposed to return to the Rehab Centre, but I couldn't because there was a virus of some kind going around.

I felt a surge of excitement run through me, because instead of going back to Rehab I was able to go home, before my special event with Nick Carter I had found out from my nurse that my mom begged the staff to keep me at the Rehab Centre for a couple weeks longer. This was sometime end of February beginning of March, I had felt a little upset because I wanted to go home. Sometime later I found out that my mom had to take my older brother Jamie to California to see our dad, my older brother didn't remember seeing our dad while he was in the Hospital. I felt very down for about half the month, until my moment with Nick Carter, then I was all smiles, during and after that special moment.

After I found out that I was going home I began to feel really good, this was near the end of March.

Therapy, School & Traveling

S ometime after I came out of the Hospital my mom decided to go get tested for the same thing I had. The results came back positive for ANTINUCLEAR AB. (ANA) I had felt mixed emotions of good & bad because she had escaped going through the same kind of treatment that I did.

So my first thought was *"She is one lucky woman"*. I give her a hug. I know that even though she didn't have to go through the same thing I did, the main thing was that she was with me throughout my hospitalization.

From the time I was home until summer I was busy getting my strength back, along with enjoying being home from the hospital. I still had my 24 hour tube feeding at night & could not walk long distances. I had to be carried to bed every night for a good couple of weeks. My mom was able to improvise on helping me sit & stand from the couch (by putting cushions on top of one another).

Since my occupational & physical therapists came to the house they would knock on the door, sometimes no one would be able to open the door right away.

One day when one of my therapists had come knocking on my front door, I was able to hear it, but I was not on the main floor to go answer the door.

I had called out "Come in!!!" from the master bedroom, where I was busy helping my mom fold laundry. I stood, up using an improv move to stand up, and looked out the bedroom door. I guess my mom knew what I was thinking because she said *"Don't go down there without me!"* I said *"Ok I won't"*, I then heard the knock at the door. Again I called out *"Come in!!!"* Again the door didn't opened.

I looked at my mom, then went over to the top of the stairs and thought 'Hmm . . . I wonder', I grabbed hold of the railing that was installed for my brother and made slow moves down the stairs. I knew my mom said *"Don't go down there without me"*. I thought 'What if they never come in, they will think we aren't home'. So I went down the stairs by myself without help.

Once I made it to the front door I opened it and said *"Hello . . ."* with a big smile. The therapist looked at me with a shocked expression, then my mom came down the stairs *"What are you doing down here?"* She demanded, *"I told you to wait for me"*, I just shrugged, saying *"Oh whatever, I'm still in one piece"*.

My mom still took me to my Doctor's appointments. That were in different locations in Barrie, Ontario, besides me getting my strength up I was excited about my growing strength, and felt excited about going back to school. It had been close to a year since I had been in a regular classroom, although I met a girl in the same class (which was Science) she had her own group of friends, so I was able to become friends with those girls for awhile.

I told them about my health. I had a book of facts as well. I asked the girls *"Have you heard of Lupus before?"* they had said. *"No, not really"* I decided to give them a little bit of a description that was self-explanatory because I figured why not educate them? I said *"Well it deals with the immune system. I have it, I was diagnosed with it a year ago."* They asked. *"Oh ok, how are you doing now?"* *"I'm doing pretty well, but I tell you, it's not fun to be in a hospital for a year."* Their reply to that made me think *"Are you insane?"* They went on. One girl said *"I would rather be in a hospital then at school."* My first thought was 'I guess they will never know what it is like to be at death's door step'.

I did my best to stay as positive as possible, my friendship with the girl in my class & her friends lasted until they told me that I was acting to much like a 'Bitch' around them.

They all thought my life was being controlled by my health (Lupus), because they had taken my positive attitude the wrong way.

After I had a fall out from the friendship with the group of girls I began to ignore them. I began to think *"You know what, if you don't know how to handle my positive attitude, then you don't deserve to have my attention"*. I ignored these girls altogether by not acknowledging them at all. I was able to get through school until about 3 weeks before Christmas, I unfortunately ended up feeling ill to the point where I had to go to the Emergency Room.

After about a week of being hospitalized I was hoping to go home by the end of the following week, but then I was told that I was to stay one more week for observation. My doctors didn't think I was up to par yet. By the end of the 3rd week I was finally able to go home and my excitement was indescribable, I was bouncing up & down in the front seat of my mom's car on the way home saying, "*I get to be home for Christmas & New Years, Woohoo*!!!".

Once the Holidays were over and done, I knew that it was time to go back to school, but every time I thought of school it made me feel really tired & depressed because of what happened before I was in the hospital before Christmas. My mom knew right away what was wrong and said "*Don't go to school, you don't have to go back*". My mom saw how sad I looked, and when she told me "*No*", I nodded and went back to sleep.

From that point on I had forgot about school and chose to focus on recuperating. Being in a hospital for such a long time can take a lot out of a person. I did receive a phone call from the school, but I don't really remember what was really talked about. When I picked up the phone the caller had said "Hello, *may I please speak to Anne-Marie Kittiphanh*." I said "*Speaking*" the caller said "*Hey there, I am from Bear Creek Secondary School*". "*Oh . . .*", I said, in a not so enthusiastic tone, the caller had picked up on it right away, cause she had said "*You don't sound very happy*" I replied "*You could say that*", I don't remember what else was said; all I know is that the call lasted 10 minutes, tops.

About a month later my mom & I were asked to speak about my experience of meeting Nick Carter through the Make-A-Wish Foundation, we had to travel to Blue Mountain for two days & one night; I was given the chance to speak about how I felt during the experience & afterwards, I was then given a copy of the taping of me backstage meeting Nick Carter at Kool Haus in Toronto.

A/N: I still have the cassette of my meet with Nick Carter.

I still have no words to express how appreciative I am to the Make-A-Wish Foundation for making my biggest wish come true, because in 1997 when I found out about Nick Carter I felt curious of him but didn't think meeting him would be possible.

Not long after that phone call I turned 18, I was feeling better. Over the summer, along with getting myself back to its normal slim shape like most girls would have, I had begun to build muscle and I looked healthy. Was more active, more like I usually was and I did my best to eat more as well. I may have still had to have a GJ-Tube feeding every night but I actually begun to look like my normal self again.

By September of 2004 I was able to get my GJ-Tube removed. Sometime later I was transferred to an Adult Lupus Doctor, they didn't want me to have the GJ-Tube in so they had given me a note of approval to have it removed. There was a lot of phone tag between myself & my Lupus Doctor on the day I was supposed to get my GJ-Tube removed. my Lupus Doctor from Sick Kids told me that I needed it to help gain my weight back to my normal weight which was 55kg (105 pounds) my weight at that time was between 45 kilos, which was 99 to 100 pounds. My body was not up to the Doctor's standards, which is why he wanted me to keep the tube in. I was advised that if the feeding tube stayed in, doctors would make sure I got enough nourishment from the tube, I wouldn't have to worry about having a feeding machine be an alarm clock early in the morning. I had the feeding tube in while I was in the hospital. I had secretly hated the fact of having a tube in my stomach.

Christmas & New Years of 2005, my family celebrated both occasions by throwing a dual party, since I was out of the hospital for most of that year. I was all dolled up, celebrating because the only time I went to the hospital was for Doctor's appointments. I was pretty well health wise, so I didn't have that many hospital stays. My 19th birthday was 2 months later and the event had lasted 2 weeks because my oldest brother Bob was absent working out of town so I was treated like royalty for 2 whole weeks pretty awesome! The first week of my birthday, I spent time with my mom, stepdad & older brother Jamie. For the 2nd week, my oldest brother Bob joined us to help finish the celebration and my entire family was able to come to together for my birthday. I did end up going to the hospital because I wasn't feeling well but I was able to leave a week after March Break ended. About three months later my mom told my oldest brother Bob to take Jamie & I to visit our dad, who was in Milwaukee Wisconsin. My brothers & I went down to the United States for a week to visit then returned to Canada. About two months later, my parents & I went on an all expense paid cruise trip compliments of my parents home based business, The *Caribbean Princess* cruise was amazing plus it was my first cruise trip. My brothers were invited however they refused to join me and our parents for the amazing experience.

They had no idea what they were missing but it was their loss for thinking that it would be no fun. I had a grand ol' time and it was worth it. About a month later my family came back together and we all travelled to Laos which is located north of Thailand. We all stayed there for two months or so.

Twentieth Birthday & Englehart

I was able to be home for Christmas once again, it was amazing to spend time with my family. It soon occurred to me that I was going to be an adult quite soon. I couldn't believe that I was going to be 20 years old. My birthday was celebrated over the course of a weekend. On Friday night I went to a potluck dinner at a friends house, on Saturday Night I went out to play mini putt with my oldest brother Bob & Stepdad Tom, and on Sunday Night I went to the movies and got to see "*Underworld: Evolution*"(its a vampire movie if you readers don't know what it is all about).

About four months later, on the first weekend of June my mom took my older brother Jamie & I up to Englehart, where all three of us kids were born & raised. My mom thought it would be a good time to test my health to see how well I could handle being up north after being away for so long. While we were up there I was able to see my best friend from High School, Annie Morrison, along with my childhood friends Shawna Holmes & Joe Milton, the two people that I would hang out with most often throughout my childhood.

It wasn't until the day we all returned from Englehart that I began to feel unwell, I had felt light headed. I was able to hold out until I sat down at the dinner table. Then I actually felt like I was going to black out while I was eating my dinner. I told my mom that I was going to bed early. The next day mom took my older brother & I out for breakfast.

It was sometime after I had my first plate of breakfast that I realised that I probably would not be able to go back up to Englehart ever again (unless I go there for a different reason). My mom asked "*Why?*" I said "*I felt dizzy the day before at dinner.*" My mom turned to me "*I'm sorry*", she said." *Its a semi-failed health test*".

Charity—Howie Dorough

N ear the end of the next week I was able to meet another member of the Backstreet Boys, it was Howie Dorough also known as Sweet D, was at a cocktail/mocktail Charity Event in Toronto at the Diesel Playhouse, almost like a nightclub kind of setting.

When I arrived there was already a line up, of people waiting at the entrance. I was able to meet different people.

I had to have my ID checked in case I was going to be drinking alcohol, and after that was done, everybody was to head upstairs where everything was located: the drinks, snacks & Charity souvenirs were all set up. I checked out the entire place, admiring everything, including the music that was playing over the speakers. I listened intently to whatever song that was being played.

After I looked around at everything I went back to stand at the top of the stairs and just watched people mingle and get to know each other. Since I had my back to the stairs, I didn't really pay attention to who else had arrived. I allowed the thoughts in my mind to wander until I felt a tap on my shoulder. I turned around to see a girl in a black strapped evening gown looking at me curiously, We looked at each other for a moment then the girl asked "*Hello . . . Do you know how much the souvenirs are??*" I looked over at the table in thought then said "*I don't really know . . . I checked out the different things but didn't really pay attention to the price*". The girl then asked "*Would you like to come with me & see how much they are??*" I looked at her and thought '*hey . . . I'm making new friends, which is awesome*' I smiled at her and said "*Sure . . . Oh my name is Anne-Marie Kittiphanh by the way,*" I said as I began walking toward the souvenirs. The girl introduced herself and said "*Cool . . . My name is Behiwot Degefu, call me Bee for short, all my friends call me Bee*".

After we made introductions of who we were, we stayed together and got to know each other. It wasn't long before Bee & I exchanged numbers & emails to keep in touch with each other. Our friendship took off from there. We talked until it was time for the mini concert.

Once we heard the announcement, we got in line, then found a seat close to the front of the stage in the small room. It was almost like attending a small comedy show that was about to commence. Bee & I had our cameras ready for the show, making sure to capture everything. The first person to make an appearance was Howie D's Protégé, his name is George Nozuka, very talented on the guitar & keyboard, and also very good looking.

Howie knew that George was going to be famous one day just like the Backstreet Boys.

Once George finished his part as an intro, Howie stepped out and the room went wild. The volume of sound in the room went from silence to music on bass boost. My ears were ringing. Once the entire room was able to quiet down to almost no sound at all, Howie explained about his sister Caroline & the development of the Dorough Lupus Foundation in her memory. It was so awesome.

After Howie explained everything about the Charity Foundation he announced that he was going to take the entire room down memory lane, singing songs from each of the Backstreet Boys Albums that the Backstreet Boys had done over the years.

The songs were the following:

> "*All I Have To Give*"—Backstreet's Back Album
> "*I Want It That Way*"—Millennium Album
> "*How Did I Fall In Love With You*"—Black &
>   Blue Album
> "*Drowning*"—The Hits: Chapter One Album
> "*Incomplete*"—Never Gone Album

During the entire song "*Drowning*", I had this image in my mind of me in the hospital in the three day coma. As soon as Howie sang the first few words of the song, I silently cried my eyes out through out the song (I began to look around hoping no one was watching me cry) Once Howie finished the song. I stopped crying in a *snap* just like that. After the mini show was done, there was the meet & greet with both Howie & George at the table that was set up by the stair case, Bee & I decided to wait and be the last to meet Howie.

While Bee & I were waiting for most of the crowd to leave Bee had encouraged me to tell Howie about my Lupus along with how one song had meant so much to me. When it was our turn I told Howie that I was there for two reasons.

Reason #1: I had been a fan of the Backstreet Boys since I was eleven years old, I am now/then twenty, even though I didn't look that old. I also told Howie that I had met Nick before as well, he said "*Cool*".

Reason #2: I had come to support the Dorough Lupus Foundation because I also had Lupus, I have had it since I was sixteen years old and I have been taking medication daily.

The year before Howie's sister Caroline passed away, that was the year that I had heard about the Backstreet Boys. Also, when Howie sang '*Drowning*', I had cried through the entire song. As soon as Howie sang the song I had this image of me in the hospital from 2002 when I was really sick. Once Howie finished the song the image was gone, I was in shock, because I didn't think that the song would mean that much to me. But until that image came up in my mind, I thought "*Oh my gosh*" I had forgotten that when I was in the hospital, I would always sing along to that one song.

I also explained to Howie how I had felt when I listened one of his songs the one that was called "*What Makes You Different (Makes You Beautiful)*", it had reminded me so much of High School because I was always pushed around & called names. Once I was done explaining how I felt, Howie said "*I'm flattered*". Howie had hugged me three times because I had cried more than once in front of him.

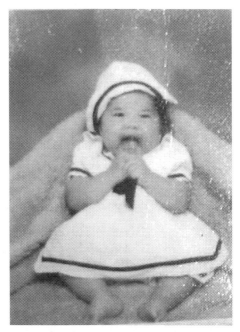

Me At 3 Months

Mom's Wedding Nov 17, '02

Aug 2001 Family & I Visiting Jamie In Rehab

Feb 2002 My Glamour Photo At Age 16

Me after grade 8 grad wearing my speech medal proudly

Me In The Hospital A Couple Months After
My 16th Birthday

April 27, 2001 Me In The Waiting Room After
Jamie's Accident

Me inside a Limo for the 1st time

Me with my mom

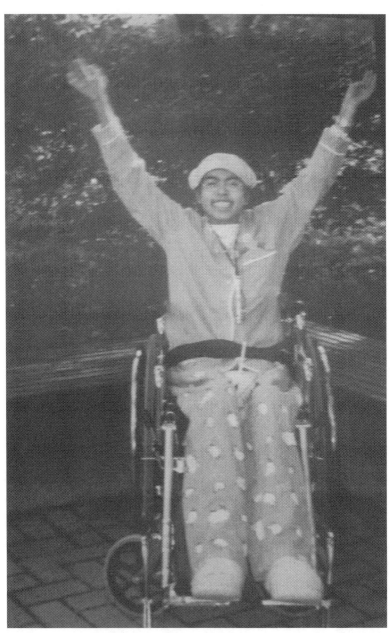

Sept 2002 Me Getting Fresh Air

Mom posing with me with jamie in the background

My 2 godmother from the Make-A-Wish Foundation

My 2nd knitting work after 4months
The Backstreet Blanket

My family visiting me in the hospital for x-mas

My 1st Trip Home From The Hospital

Me At Grade 8 Graduation Dance With A Friend

Me Meeting Nick Carter Backstage At Kool Haus

Me hugging Nick Carter

Me hugging Nick Carter while sitting down

Nick Carter pointing at me at his solo concert

Me meeting Howie D at the Diesel Playhouse in T.O.

Myspace. Pneumonia & Charity

About a month later at around the second week of July I began chatting with someone that claimed were related to my Favourite Backstreet Boy Nick Carter, I had had my doubts and should have kept it only to end up crying for a half hour which isn't nice. Next time I would remember that if someone says they are someone they are not, to never believe them cause it will just ruin a persons day, although its a lesson learned.

I had then checked out a website called "*Myspace*" I actually got to see the profile of my Favourite Backstreet Boy Nick Carter on the website, I was unsure whether to join although I wanted to try and keep in contact with him so I figured why not become a member of the "*Myspace*" website. So I became a member of "*Myspace*" and checked out different other sites that had graphics to add to the page. It took me a good week to figure out how to make it look nice then I added my Favourite Backstreet Boy Nick

Carter. It wasn't long before I received a blog update by Nick Carter himself via *"Myspace"*, I felt in shock and said *"OH MY GOD"*. It took me a good thirty minutes before I was able to calm down. It never occurred to me that I wasn't the only one receiving the same blog update.

I found out during the second week of September from my mom that I didn't have to worry about getting PCP Pneumonia anymore, because I had been clean for 3 years. I actually felt like a weight had been lifted off my shoulders. It was interesting of how I was told the news about it, it will even make you chuckle a little bit.

I was having a nap one day and my mom had come in to see what was on TV in my room. I was feeling a little groggy since I was resting *"Mom what do you want"* I asked and mom said *"You don't have to go to the Hospital on the 13 of this month"* I had said *"Really?"*, I asked, *"When did you find this out? Did the Doctor call??"* *"Yes,"* my mom said *"The Doctor just called saying they have cancelled the appointment"*.

I felt briefly happy cause I thought 'Yahoo! no more Sick Kids!' since I didn't have to go to Sick Kids anymore! But at the same time I felt relieved because then I didn't have to worry about juggling appointments with other appointments anymore, I felt very happy about the news of not having PCP Pneumonia anymore.

Even though I knew that I didn't have PCP Pneumonia, I felt slight sadness cause I wouldn't get to visit my former nurses from Sickkids anymore; I really enjoyed how well I was taken care of by however many nurses that I had had when I was a patient there, on the other hand I was able to relax & enjoy recuperating at home.

My Lupus S.L.E was doing better and getting more quieter & quieter as time went by. All there was left was wait and find out when I needed to see my Lupus Doctor again.

I still had to be poked for blood work every week. Then the pokes went from every week to every second week, cause I was put on a medication injection that dealt with a blood clot on my left arm.

About two months later I found out that Howie D of the Backstreet Boys was going to be hosting another Lupus Charity event, this time in New York I had asked my mom if she would be willing to go with me. I was relieved to find out that it was going to be a girl's trip to the Big City of New York. My mother & I went to the Big City with two of our close friends that were also a mother & daughter.

We had decided to drive rather than buy a place ticket but it was a very fun adventure for all of us, at the border between Canada and the States. My mom's friend told her daughter and myself to stay quiet because if we all spoke at the same time it would be very confusing for the people at the toll booth.

Once we drove up to the toll booth we all ended up doing what we were specifically told not to do which was talk all at once. In all honesty it was the funniest moment of the entire road trip.

You would wonder why a group of two mothers & daughters embarking on a road trip to the United States would really make you laugh for a good while before you realise what the real reason is of the road trip was. It wasn't long before we made it to the Big City. It took awhile for us all to find our hotel, since it was located a little bit outside of Manhattan (the inner part of New York).

We were able to find the hotel & get settled in and the next day we all took a shuttle to the inner part of New York. Once we got there, we spent pretty much the whole day walking, trying to find the location of the Lupus Charity Event. It turned out that it was in Jay-Z's 40/40 Club. Once we found the location we soon realised that a movie was being filmed at the same location, and just when my mom thought she never get to see any other Celebrity, we all noticed a car drive up on the opposite side of the street.

Who do we all see inside a vehicle driving up? Is none other than Will Smith (The Fresh Prince of Bel-Air) himself. Since my mom had the digital camera, she was able to capture the entire thing. I was able to shake Will Smith's hand. My gosh is he ever tall! My mom was able to capture him up close on video.

After Will Smith left we all went back to the entrance of Jay-Z's 40/40 Club where the Charity Event was going to be held. We all had the chance to explore the Club itself, like a private tour. It was interesting. The Lupus Event began and we headed to the room where the lupus event and everything was going to take place.

While we were all waiting for the host to arrive I was able to meet another fan of the Backstreet Boys, Jahaira Maisonet, She told me that she was a huge fan of the host which was pretty awesome.

Soon we all began to hear people whisper '*He is here, the host is here.*' I looked around and there standing by the entrance of the room was Howie D, I could see him from the far corner where I was sitting in the room. I waved at him and he waved back. It wasn't long before I was encouraged to go talk to Howie about my gift to the group my new friend Jahaira or Jay as I call her told me I should go to Howie and tell him about my gift that I had made. While I was in the hospital my mom had brought a bag of wool & knitting needles during her visits, I used it to my advantage and began making 20x20 squares I was able to make blankets. The first blanket was made for my parents business team it was very rough, and the second one was dedicated to The Backstreet Boys, my gift to them for making amazing music.

I was encouraged to ask Howie if he had remembered me, then to tell him about the blanket that I had brought with me. Since I am a shy person, I was unsure how to go about talking to Howie again. However I chose to set aside my nerves and just went cause I thought *'Eh . . . why not'*. I got up and walked over to Howie and said *"Do you remember me . . . From Toronto, the Diesel Playhouse?"* he said *"Yeah, I do remember"* and gave me a hug, I then proceeded to tell him that I had something to give him. I explained that I was there with my mom and our close friends and that we were all in the far corner of the room, not long after that my mom & her friend brought my backpack over with the gift.

Once I had the backpack I pulled out the blanket that I had made and held it up for everybody to see, I had said *"While I was in the hospital for so long I began to do knitting, this is what I came up with for my second project since I had done one before. I wanted to make something for The Backstreet Boys and dedicate it to the group for making amazing music, this is a gift from my heart to the hearts of the Backstreet Boys"*.

While I was explaining about the blanket, there were camera flashes from every direction by everybody that had attended the Charity Event.

I then went back to sit down after about fifteen minutes of camera flashes cause I knew the event was about a fundraiser, I didn't want to steal the spotlight from Howie cause it was his Charity Event for Lupus. I sat down for about say twenty minutes before I realised that everybody was gathered around the covered pool tables with different silent auction items, I had noticed my friend Jay standing by the pool table and I was wondering why so I stood up and went over and stood beside Jay.

I looked over to my right and there, mere inches from me, was Howie D! I was practically rubbing my arm against his, standing that close to him I just couldn't believe it! I had such a good time. When I had to leave to catch the shuttle bus I was a little sad that I had to leave earlier than I wanted. But I was able to do what I wanted, which was give Howie D The Backstreet Blanket while at the Lupus Charity Event. I felt like I had no choice but to leave with my mom, so I left with my mom & our close friends to where the shuttle bus was going to pick us up.

The next day we all headed back to Canada, our time in the Big City was a blast, yet short.

Christmas & Mom's Health

For Christmas 2006 my family & I had a huge party, so in other words it was a full house so lots & lots of people. I was able to make a few friends which was pretty awesome I became a hostess for a couple of girls that I became fast friends with that were there with their parents, I was able to entertain them with movies that were on my computer that was a desktop at the time.

Before the party ended I made sure to exchange email addresses with them so that they & I could keep in touch, the girls names were Jocelyn & Alexia (Lexxie for short) I became really good friends with them. My health was fine through out January of 2007 until sometime in the first few weeks of February I began to feel like I was catching a flu or a head cold, the symptoms I had lasted two weeks although two weeks before I was able to witness what happens when a person goes through a stroke.

The good thing was that it wasn't me, it was my mom that had to be taken to the Emergency room by Ambulance, it turned out that my mom had had a mini-stroke I was able to ride along with my mom in the Ambulance sitting in the front passenger seat. It was interesting how two people's roles can be switched around by just one single situation, because it would usually be myself on the stretcher either unconscious or asleep.

I had stayed with my mom the entire time in the ER, that evening I was wearing dark blue tracksuit and its pretty funny cause I was mistaken as a Hospital Staff so a Nurse that was working there. I never left my mom's bedside most of the time when she was going through tests. The date was March 4.

Luckily my mom didn't have to spend the night and we were able to go home later that evening. My mom still had tests done to investigate & see what was wrong. After a while my mom had to wear a machine on her chest to monitor her heart rate in case she had another stroke, my mom had already had 40+ other tests done on her.

On one of her tests it showed that my mom had bone cancer. The last weekend of March she had sent me to a seminar dealing with tons of beauty products, I was fine for about five minutes writing notes except I couldn't concentrate because of feeling worried about my mom. The one & only thing that came to my mind was '*I can't imagine my life without my mom*', by the time the seminar was done I was crying my eyes out.

It wasn't long after I had my emotional breakdown about my mom's diagnosed bone cancer. I was down to my last dose of prednisone the date was Friday April 13, 2007.

Fund-Raising, Family Feud & Debate

Sometime later I received a message from a lady who was preparing a fundraiser for Lupus. It was cool that they were a Lupus Supporter, so I figured why not reply and become friends? The lady's name is Trudy, she & I began chatting and I was able to explain that I had Lupus. We also talked about hobbies and all the different things that deals with a friendship.

I also found out that Trudy is a mother with a Thyroid Disorder in her thirties, married with two children named Christopher & Megan, and they all lived in Trenton, Ontario, I also found out that Trudy & her son Christopher are also huge fans of The Backstreet Boys. I was curious of who were their favourite members out of the group, it turned out that Trudy is a huge fan of Howie D & Trudy's son Christopher is a huge fan of Nick Carter.

I had explained to Trudy that I was able to meet Howie D twice the previous year, shared my experience with being able to meet Howie D & everything. After I shared my two experiences Trudy explained to me about what she was doing which was a Lupus fundraiser called "*Wild Life Walk For Lupus*". Trudy asked me to help her in arranging & preparing everything that dealt with the fundraiser.

Since I was providing a lot of life experience of having the Challenge along with information in what I was going through, I thought '*Hey . . . Why not, I have been wanting to share my experience in some way or another*' so I had agreed to go along and Trudy invited me to stay with her at her house for 2 1/2 weeks (even though I had absolutely no idea what their living & sleeping arrangements were there). In terms of whose idea it was for me to stay there was all Trudy's it was never mine; I had agreed thinking it was an amazing, marvellous idea, it wasn't until I got there that things went from ok to '*what the heck was I thinking?*' kind of idea.

While I was still getting to know Trudy, she had also told me about her fear of the fictional character "*Jason*", I had made the mistake of telling my family about Trudy's fear rather than explaining that Trudy is a huge Lupus Supporter, that was on me and my fault. (Since I was still learning to handle situations I wasn't acting in the proper way to deal with the good or bad circumstances). Since I had talked about Trudy's fear my family didn't like it very much and I don't blame them for feeling the way they did. It turned out Trudy had a pretty good life before her present circumstances.

Trudy & I kept chatting via IM & phone since I had given Trudy my number the evening that Trudy had arrived at my house my mom prepared a huge feast with fancy dishes & everything, Trudy had brought most of her family to meet mine and that same night I was able to meet the rest of Trudy's family and her mother.

Trudy had a pretty good life with her own family because before relocating to her mother's house, they were living in a basement apartment that had polished hardwood furniture & everything. It wasn't until one day the basement apartment got flooded & ruined everything, so Trudy & her family had no choice but to relocate and move in with her mother which was a house that could be from the 60's or 70's with three small bedrooms, one bathroom & an unfinished basement that was filled from floor to ceiling with all of small family's belongings (honestly, whatever she could fit in such a small place all at once).

I was surprisingly able to adapt fairly quickly, although the word *"cramped"* would be a huge understatement, in terms of how this family could live in that kind of setting was beyond me. The one thing that I was not expecting was after I had arrived there was the amount of arguing that had went on between Trudy and her family, I thought they were a pretty close knit family my guess is that Trudy's idea for a Lupus Fundraiser didn't quite go well between Trudy & her family.

For the 2 1/2 weeks that I had stayed there I found out that Trudy had asked for help from her family for about the same amount of time I was in the hospital for (meaning as in the timeline), Trudy was hoping for help & support from her entire family to only end up getting nothing in return.

It turned out that I was Trudy's only hope. Another thing that I never thought I would be witness of was how much Trudy argued with her mother about anything & everything under the sun. One of my fears in life besides plastic eight legged creatures would be loud angry voices and voice of Trudy's mom had a volume of a million at once in a gigantic stadium (think of a sold out stadium filled with people screaming for their favourite singer it was that loud) because I remember the last time I heard her voice it made my ears ring to where I almost cried my eyes out.

As for sleeping arrangements lets just say its less than pleasant although I did my best to show that everything was fine. Trudy & her daughter slept on a medium sized thick mattress on the living room floor, her son Christopher slept on the couch & her husband Michael slept in the basement, I, of course, slept in the living room beside Trudy & her daughter.

You would think that any of the rooms in the house would be vacant for a guest room since there were three bedrooms. It turns out that one of the rooms was made up as an office; the remaining two bedrooms were small but they were used for sleeping. Since Trudy didn't have a Job at the time the only person that was able to pay for the wireless Internet bill was her husband Michael, because he did different moving jobs around the area. There was in fact a small little trailer that belonged to Trudy's mother, it was parked at the end of the driveway at the back of the house.

Besides having to be around Trudy & her mother arguing, I was like a deer caught in headlights I had no idea what to do or think, I kept my distance, not wanting to be caught in the cross fire within a family. Even though the fights were never about me I had no other choice but to watch and listen to each & every fight that went on between Trudy & her family, I had volunteered to help out with arranging a Lupus Fundraiser, not get involved with a family that were at all odds with each other about everyday normal things!

All Trudy had asked from her family was help to plan & arrange everything for a Lupus Event doesn't sound so hard if you really think about it, Trudy & her family weren't on the same wavelength because of the countless disagreements that were made left & right I wondered how can this family put on an event that is so disorganized? *'does this family not want to support a cause especially when they have a guest that has gone through the experience of what is being supported?'* Of course I didn't voice my thought since I was a guest not anything more than that.

There was also hopes of me not having to end up in hospital there in Trenton. I ended up getting flea or bug bites because I was unable to stop scratching my ankles & shoulders so I had to get taken to the ER of the hospital in Trenton, Ontario.

By the fourth night I was told to stay in the trailer of Trudy's mother, I don't know what was worse having to worry about itchy red spots or being caught in the cross fire of a whole lot of Family Feud of a family I was visiting. I understand that family can have fights about a lot of different things, but to have a guest be brought in and have them witness what has been going on for a long time, its almost like making your own family look bad by refusing to get along because of not supporting what the guest has gone through in their life.

Its amazing how one person is able & willing to help out a friend only to have that person's family give off negative vibes when it should be positive. Truthfully I didn't get much help either with trying to get everything organized when I was bothered so much. It's not easy. I thought that children in a family would have something to do besides bother the guest that was trying to do something for a worthy cause, Trudy's son would do things without a care in the world and Trudy didn't do much, just allowed him to do whatever since it was their house.

They seemed like such nice people, that is until you spend time with them on their grounds then its anything goes. I know not all people are like that. However if you have a problem with a family that is not on the same wavelength you need to get out of it. I understand they are family, but why not try to get along for the sake of the guest rather than making the guest feel like they shouldn't even be there?

In terms of making sure I ate, that's a little hard to explain without making you think I wasn't treated with respect or consideration. There was plenty of food everywhere in certain parts of the house, except it was for one person only so (in other words this stash is his & this stash is hers "*Hands Off*") I was able to do what I could without saying anything, in case I would set someone off. Trudy had taken me grocery shopping except I have no idea what happened to what we had bought, because her son Christopher or her brother Carl would be all over it.

As for me speaking at all you can say it was nothing at all. I had no idea how to handle this family in terms of what I needed because when things were quiet I was afraid to say anything. Having to be brought into a family that were at all odds with each other was one thing, however not being asked if I was hungry or if I was comfortable would be a whole different situation altogether.

I was never asked if I was hungry, if I needed anything or if I was comfortable, absolutely nothing of sort with this family, yet I had volunteered my expertise about something that this family had refused to support. I felt like I had no choice but to think like every person for them self so I looked for anything that was easy, I understood that it wasn't right however I thought it was better than setting someone off the edge of getting upset.

I was advised *"Don't touch any of the food you see around the house, because its spoken for"* kind of thing. As for the food from the grocery store, it went from being put away one day then gone the next. With the kind of situation I was in, I had to think of a way to get what I needed, I was to scared to ask Trudy for anything because she was on edge about her mother.

As for anything for me to drink, it wasn't a problem, the problem was just making sure I was able to have enough food to eat. With Lupus a person needs to rest. That would be another need, where respect & consideration comes in. I never got it from Trudy's son. I was able to lie down in the trailer, except peace didn't come as easily. Once I was able to get to sleep, I'd be woken up unexpectedly by Christopher banging on the side of the trailer.

In terms of good kids I figure they would be good mannered. of course in this case it was their grounds, so if the kids want to make their presence known, they will. There was a point where I wanted to rest except I had felt so tired & exhausted that as much as I wanted rest I knew I wouldn't get it, I was in the trailer and Trudy came in to where I was and I was doing my best to not show my emotions that in itself was not easy.

As for the planning, planning for the Fundraiser never got completed because of the arguing back & forth, along with a lot of psychological humiliation that I had to go through. A host is supposed to make sure the guest is comfortable and able to help get things done, not keep arguing with those that refused to support an idea and not bother with how the guest was feeling throughout the entire situation. My mom had called a few times to check up on me along with tell me to go home, there was no way I was going to tell my mom & family that the family I agreed to help wasn't on the same wavelength as Trudy & myself (of course once they read this they will think its my fault, honestly I was trying to help Trudy as well as make sure I was able to get through Trudy's situation with my dignity intact not make things worse).

When I had went home I made sure to act like everything was normal & fine, I refused to talk about how a family can fight about a worthy cause with my family knowing that if they knew I would had to explain why I agreed to help in the first place. I still kept in contact with Trudy via IM & phone, since the day for the actual Fundraiser was still ahead. Of course Trudy hoped that the Co-Founder of another Lupus Foundation would be able to attend except she didn't have much luck with that.

It wasn't long before I realised that Trudy had invited me back to go camping during the Event of her Lupus Fundraiser, the funny thing was that Trudy's husband

Michael never decided to help out until the day or night before the Event was to take place. I was able to help Trudy set up camp and everything else, of course there are different ways to camp the usual comfortable way or roughed we of course roughed it and I did my best to keep warm.

The last thing Trudy & I both needed was to be late on the Big Day of the Fundraiser, but it turns out she & I had accidentally slept in and were forty-five minutes late. Can't really blame us when its so cold at half past six a.m. I was scrambling so much that I almost lost that day's medication down the drain (yea . . . not good). Trudy was able to have Canopies set up since it was on a beach, the planning may not have been completely finished however the Event did fairly well Trudy & I were able to raise over $500 dollars or $5,000 dollars with a bit of change that day.

I did my best to keep a good front since it was a nice day. At Trudy's it was back to 'every person for themselves'. I was sent to get food, only I had returned with enough for myself, of course I get told off by Trudy's neighbour saying I wasn't thinking of anyone else but myself. If anyone has ever thought of what its like to be told or looked at as like 'being selfish' oh I won't go there since its just not even worth elaborating on.

I may have been the guest to this event; in truth my presence didn't mean anything to anyone except Trudy, but since Trudy was busy keeping the different other events controlled I think she may had forgotten that I was even there. Having to be on the go since half past 6 that morning, I felt exhausted. And knowing how I was treated by Trudy's family a couple months before was pretty much like 'stay away'.

There was no way I was going to ask for anything.

Its interesting because Trudy's family may have refused to help organise the Event, but they were more than willing to help clean up. Funny how that is, besides having being told off about having my own peanut butter sandwich, much to my surprise the first real meal of that day was having pizza for dinner. After everything that I tried to do to help with organizing a Fundraiser, there was no apology from Trudy or any of her family about them all arguing about the Fundraiser especially when I had offered to share my story I didn't receive much in return.

You wouldn't believe where I had ended up after the Fundraiser ended three days later I had to be taken to the ER because of a high fever of 104.8 degrees Fahrenheit. As I sat in the ER with my stepdad, trying my best to stay awake, I knew that what I had gone through was the cause of my fever, because I never drank anything during the Fundraiser and I was pretty much told I was selfish for thinking of my own stomach. Try being put in a situation where its *"think for yourself, don't worry"* only to be put in a position where you are like *"in the right place, at the wrong time"*.

I was lucky enough to not have to spend the night however. The estimated time I was in the ER at that time was 8 hours, I was in at 3:00 pm and I never left until 11:00 pm, a long time for one person to wait. Of course I was able to talk to Trudy the next day and explained what happened after the Fundraiser, as for how Trudy reacted it wasn't *"I'm glad you feel better"* or *"Next time we will do something different"* as well as *"Thank you for your time & sharing your story with us"* or *"I'm happy we did the*

Fundraiser together, it was a little hectic but I hope we can do it again" nothing at all along those lines.

The response I received from Trudy was "Will *you be willing to come to my next Wild Life Walk for Lupus??*", all I could say was "*I'll see what I can do, I can't promise anything*".

Earlier that same year I did a survey for the Dorough Lupus Foundation, I was unsure whether to tell Trudy or not yet the idea popped up while I was staying with Trudy that first time. The survey was about a Lupus Charity Cruise that was going to set sail at the end of that year, Trudy & I had agreed to book cabins together.

I soon found out that my mom was leaving Canada for Health Reasons, my mom agreed to pay for my Cruise in advance so that there wouldn't be any problems. When I told Trudy about what my mom was doing for me her specific words were "*Your mom has nothing to do with the Cruise*", of course my mom over heard it and I just looked at my mom with an expression that said "*Just pay for the ticket, send me off & pray that I get back home in one piece*". I was doing my best to keep Trudy at bay while handling my mom leaving Canada & paying for my Cruise ticket all at once.

Then there was another problem how I would get to the port from my place of residence. I was asked by Trudy to take the Greyhound bus but my family wanted me to take the plane, so you can see what kind of position I was in I was doing my best to answer Trudy's plea while making my decision.

In the end I chose to fly to the port rather than take the Greyhound bus, Trudy may not have liked my choice of transportation at least I made it to the Cruise & back in one piece.

Of course after I came back from the Cruise the weather changes from boiling hot to freezing cold. That can affect a person, especially one that has absolutely no immune system to fight off infections. I was on the couch for two weeks groggy and in pain from the drastic weather change. It took me another full week to get back on my feet. Its amazing what a life threatening illness can do to one person alone especially when it comes to huge temperature changes.

Deciding, Reducing & Pass
Slow and Steady

After the Charity Cruise I spent the next several months trying to sort out what to do with my schooling, I always wanted to finish school because of being taken out of the 9th Grade level early. I had wanted to get my education back for a while but of course my health was preventing me from doing so, I had no choice but to wait for my health to let me know whether it was ok for me to return again.

I knew the only thing holding me back was my education for a long time, whatever I was planning for my future I knew I had to get as much of my education back as possible. My stepdad suggested that I attend a School called The Barrie Literacy Council, a place where adults are able to excel in their Reading, Writing & Math Skills I felt unsure about the place at first but then thought

'*Hey . . . If this is a start to getting my education back then by all means*'.

I wanted to upgrade my Math skills a bit since I knew that I was quite weak in that area, I had surprised myself by going from a mid-week Class to an early-week Class. I even had a Tutor for the summer, my Tutor was able to help me with a Writing Problem called run ons like a means to a '*No*' end kind of thing.

I had a Tutor for the entire summer of 2008, while I was still going to Classes I was able to attend two BSB Concerts they were amazing I wasn't able to attend any Concerts in the past. I still went to Doctor's appointments and my last was on December 9, 2008 I was advised to stop taking five medications, at that time I was on seven taking five away meant that I was down to two which was pretty amazing I would have been on three but I can get Calcium from anything so I was on Vitamin D & Lisinopril.

I went from taking medication three times a day to once a day which was very awesome I chose to change the time which was as soon as I woke up, it's so that I wouldn't have to worry about it for the rest of the day. It's astounding that I went from twenty-two different medications three times a day to two medications once a day, in a span of six years it's just amazing.

I enjoyed attending school because I had come a long way in a short time if you think about it, I went from going to The Barrie Literacy Council and was transferred to The Barrie Learning Centre within a span of eight months. I went from a place of upgrading to a place where Adults are able to achieve what was left of their Schooling, for those that were able to get the remaining credits that were left behind because of life getting in the way.

I was able to learn how to do a PowerPoint (PPT) slideshow I made my own slideshow in one day which was pretty good, my stepdad explained to me that I am a quick learner when it came to new things which was a pretty nice compliment.

The first Course of the term I was in a debate of what topic to do my assignment on, the teacher said to do something that made me feel comfortable. I was going back & forth between doing it on drugs or alcohol I don't know why I chose two it was just first ideas that came up, I was going to do my assignment on both except I found out that there wasn't much to do on alcohol so I ended up doing it on drugs instead.

It made sense since I was taking drugs just not the street kind, days later I announced that I was going to do my assignment on Nick Carter. I found out that he was diagnosed with a heart condition called *"Cardiomyopathy"*, my source was from a Facebook Group titled *"Support Nick Carter"* I read the information and was shocked to find out in the *'Fine Print'* *"Nick Carter had been experiencing chest pains back in Spring 2008"* I mean the timing of finding this out could not have come at a better time.

I read on and found out that it was during the last tour for the BSB I had never felt in shock until that moment, I decided to buy the Magazine that the story was printed in to get more insight on the entire story of Nick Carter's Health Issue I purchased the Magazine the day it came out which was the end of the first week that the Course began. I was nearly in tears by the time I finished reading the entire article I knew what it was like to go through being diagnosed with something as serious & life threatening as what he was going through, I was relieved to find out that he was able to catch the problem early before it got worse for him because if he didn't . . .

I Do Not Want To Go There . . .

I found the perfect candidate for my assignment, Nick Carter and his health issue, mostly on what he was putting in his system like most people when it came to getting rid of a medical ailment except it was the hard core street drugs. He may have been the star in my assignment I chose to research others as well to give people an idea that certain Celebrities have the ability to turn to the worst possible chemicals in the world to get through problems, I was very shocked to find out that the best known actors & actresses and a few pretty good singers have the actual brains to go for something as dumb as allowing themselves to be lead under the influence of hard drugs.

I knew that the Rebel of the BSB A. J. Mclean was involved with drugs but I had absolutely no idea that Nick Carter was doing the same thing as well, I soon understood why, I don't know what I would have done if I knew what was wrong a long time ago.

For my assignment I did a PowerPoint (PPT) & Flyers on the Celebrities that I did research on, I did a fairly good job I managed to get a 68 percent on my mid-term Report Card even though during the Course I wasn't feeling well and ended up staying home for a whole week.

I knew that when I don't feel well I don't really do much, although that didn't stop me from getting my assignment done I was able to prepare my presentation & make the Flyers before presentation deadline.

I do have the tendency to over work myself I have the habit of working vigorously for a long time without a break, my brain has a bad habit of showing me 10 different ideas at once that aren't important to an actual task that I am already doing in the process.

I vaguely remember submitting a piece of writing that I had done in the past it was through The Barrie Literacy Council the program was called "*Little Women Transitions/ Transformations*", it was published in the 2008-09 issue I thought I did a good job considering that it was my first time submitting anything to anyone. There was a scheduled conference only I never went for it because it costed quite a lot of money, I did receive a certificate for participating which was better than nothing at all.

I was busy with two classes a day going through an upgraded Math Class then a half hour lunch break then Literacy Class, talk about a busy morning for one person but I was able to handle it since it kept me busy. I was able to do a good job on the Daily Math Tests my first percentage was low but not bad it had been 56%, my last Math Test was between 96 and 100% so my time spent at The Barrie Literacy Council was well worth it.

I practiced my Math skills and have fun with my Tutor for the summer, I was able to prove my teacher wrong when it came to a solving a word problem that moment had been quite humorous to say the least. The assignment was about predicting a certain time of where a person should be on a schedule, I was able to excel in my multiplication skills and was called a Math Wizard while playing a game of Multiplication Bingo . . .

Was That ever Fun!!!

My second Class seemed a little boring but I did the best I could with the time I had, I did PLAR (prior learning assessment and recognition) Exams I thought I was supposed to do five except when I arrived to do the first Exam it never occurred to me that I only had to do four instead. My name was on the list but I didn't have to take that particular Exam which was cool with me.

I was unsure what to do for the Summer so I chose to register for a Summer School Course which was Math (Workplace), I wasn't planning on going to College or University so I figured why not try it. I managed to get through Junior PLAR in the previous term so I signed up for Senior PLAR which doesn't begin until Fall 2009 to Summer 2010, I was told that it would have been my last year until I was advised otherwise.

I was advised that I wouldn't Graduate until June 2010 so in other words I had a long way to go, I was able to do Volunteering and turned it into Community Service cause I figured 'Why not, it wouldn't hurt'. I always wanted to go back to School because I wanted to finish, it has been a long time plus I was taken out at such a young age if it wasn't for my stepdad I probably would not have been doing anything, most days I wouldn't be doing much but then I would be busy with Summer School and, most likely still have to deal with two classes a day.

I was able to get through most of the Summer School Course until a week before it ended, I was sent to the office because I was caught copying off of another students work. While I was in the office the person that coordinates the programs in the School didn't believe that it was possible for me to achieve my Grade 12 Diploma, I was told to do volunteering somewhere instead.

I ended up going home and having a huge emotional meltdown, I chose to stop with School from August 2009 - February 2011.

I was still taking medication but mostly in the morning, only throughout 2011 I was doing my best to get off of the medication cause it dealt with my Kidney's & I've always wanted to get off all the medications that I was taking.

While I was getting back to School I was able to find out what its like to teach an actual class since my mom had told me once that she pictured me as being a teacher (not sure if its for an Elementary or Secondary School teacher though, just a teacher cause I was good with kids), since the course I was taking for 2011 was called "*Navigating The Workplace*" I had asked my teacher if I could teach the class about Health & knowing that I went through the medical system with my Lupus S.L.E. why not educate them; here is the thing the Secondary School that I was attending was for Adults, so I was educating Adults about my Health & what I went through.

I was able to teach the class for about half an hour along with had them guess my age since I looked like I should be in a Secondary School for teenagers not Adults, I had explained what I went through of what to do & what not to do when you go through a Health issue in life; I also explained about being an aspiring Published Author after finishing School, once I finished teaching & my class was able to guess my age I felt a little winded and doing my best to calm myself down.

Near the end of the Course I was able to experience what goes on in the ER of my local Hospital, I was able to see what kind of treatment people receive after going through different accidents on any normal day; the whole time I was supposed to ask questions if I was unsure about something, only I never did cause even though I had hoped to be a Registered Nurse—it was to be one for a different part of a Hospital not the ER so its a little different.

I had received a 72% for the course, in other words I had passed.

By the time exams came around I was pulled into the Office of the School again, I was told again that it wasn't possible for me to achieve my Grade 12 Diploma.

I ended up leaving feeling down because I was told to stop bothering with School, so I went home to nearly black out 3 times while having a rest I felt so upset. It wasn't until I chose to fight back by emailing the principal of the School explaining why I wanted to achieve my Grade 12 Diploma, 2 days later I had received 2 voice mail on my cell phone; one from the Secretary & one from the Guidance Counsellor of the School, both letting me know to be in Class at 9am on Monday.

I was in Class for the entire week before choosing to throw myself into Correspondence English for an entire month (I was asked to look after my mother since she was out of the country & returned early because she ended up getting sick somehow), I was able to finish the

Correspondence English & passing the exam for it & received a 75% which was a good thing except that I had felt completely exhausted it was all throughout the Summer. Once Fall came around I went in to speak to the Guidance Councillor of the School who then asked me *"Would you like to return to Full-Time Day School?"* and my response to that was "You are a Godsend, I would love to come back for Full-Time Day School"; cause when I first began at the Adult High School I was attending Full-Time Day School, which were classes from 9am-3:15pm with a 30minute lunch break Monday-Friday, I was hyped to return to 2 classes a day for however long.

The entire time I was dealing with being on & off of the Lisinopril throughout 2011, while dealing with 2 classes a day. From Sept 2011 - Feb 2012 I was doing pretty well in school, I was in courses where I was in a computer lab all day. The courses were English & Adventures in World History, the English part of the course was fairly simple since it dealt with writing I received a 69%; the Adventures in World History part of the course I was able to do an assignment on the late Martial Arts Master Bruce Lee along with look into my parents religious culture which was Buddhism just a little bit—I even did my final project on my parents country which is 'Laos' and the Final Mark I received was a 68%.

By this point I had 22 credits & needed 7 more in order to achieve my Grade 12, I was beyond excited because it meant I was almost done High School as an Adult; only I ended up getting faced with complications psychologically where I had ended up in the ER 3 times. I had to stop School for about 10 months before I was able to return to obtain my last remaining 7 credits, I was lucky enough to get through an entire month doing an Environmental Science Course while dealing with 7 different other assignments which were Evident Sheets for Senior Mature PLAR (I was able to get through the Evidence Sheets before the Christmas Holiday began).

Throughout 2012 while dealing with psychological complications I was able to get myself assigned to a local Lupus Doctor (rather than traveling an hour for appointments), along with getting myself assigned a local Kidney Doctor & get put on the lowest possible dose of Kidney medication which was/is 2.5MG every night cause I was always taking the medication as soon as I got up. I was also able to move into my own apartment before being able to return to School for the remaining 7 credits to finish.

By the time 2013 arrives I would have finished and be Graduating with a Grade 12 Diploma, only I would have to wait til the end of June for the Ceremony. The last course I did from Dec 3, '12 - Jan 29, '13 was Environmental Science, on top of that I had to fill out Evidence Sheets for Mature/SR PLAR. I was able to find out what my Final Mark for the course was, I had received a 63%; I passed slow and steady through everything that I did in school, it may have taken me longer to achieve but as people say *"better late than never"*.

My next Lupus appointment is Fall of 2013, my next Kidney appointment is sometime before the summer of 2013 (I hope to be off of medication some time soon, I really & truly don't want to be on any medication anymore).

My goal had always been to Graduate and get my Grade 12 and become an Inspirational Speaker, I would love to travel around the world spreading hope & Inspiration who need it most. I was the type of person that would want anything & everything for myself, except since my diagnosed Lupus I have been wanting to give back to those who are in need of hope & inspiration in their own life.

To those who think that life means nothing to live for; I have something to say to those types of people. Everybody has a purpose in life it doesn't matter who you are there are special gifts of something in everybody.

Reminiscing, Thoughts & Feelings

During the time that I was in the hospital I wrote lot of Diary entry's about my day, mostly how I felt when I had the G-Tube in because I had it in for a long time I had even wrote of my nightly dreams that I was able to remember the next morning. Most of my dreams were about me & the BSB, my mom, other times the entry's were so confusing they were hard to explain.

Most of my dreams were about Nick Carter & the BSB, half of the entry's were about how I felt every day since having diagnosed with a Health Challenge, the first entry that I wrote was about my Dad, some were about when I would meet new friends. How disappointed I would get about, not being able to see my friends from my High School back where I grew up.

Most of the time I'd try not to think about what I was going through other times I wished I never got diagnosed with Lupus S.L.E, then I would realise that there was nothing I could have done to prevent getting diagnosed. I did have my regrets from the past except I was told that I should thank God for what I have been given, because there would be a reason for everything.

I never thought that I would get diagnosed with anything, I just thought that maybe I would be able to get through life without any Health Challenge or issues.

Things happen to a person or people that they have no control over . . .

My Diary entry's I felt like it was the only place for me to let out how I was feeling without anyone knowing, I vaguely remember a Diary entry while I was in the hospital for a week in 2004. I wrote a lot of stuff while I was recuperating I never thought it would be handy until that time when I decided to let it all out . . . *to get my words out* . . .

Hopefully people will understand or will try to understand what I went through, not many people would know how it really truly feels to be in the hospital or even at home. My family never even knew what I was really feeling maybe this book will help them understand how I really felt during that time, I knew that people wanted to know my feelings & everything else except I kept it in for a reason. I never thought it would be the right time I figured I would be able to get my feelings out, not everything would be easy so I figured 'Why not write a book, my mom suggested that I could probably write a book about how much I went through'.

I never thought I'd have the courage to start until after I met a Celebrity that understood what I was going through, knowing his older sister had passed away from something similar. Except his sister had Lupus Cancer I realised that I could inspire people with what I had, not just of what I went through more of how I can get people to understand that faith in God, love in family along with inspiring people can help a person get through the most toughest times.

Now Onto My Diary Entry's . . .

Some are long & some are short but all, are of my thoughts of how I felt and the dreams that I had . . . Enjoy!!!

Realize, Think Back and Future Look

What surprised me was that I went from a 9th Grade High School student to laying in a hospital bed with a disease that I should not have had to live with to the way I am now. I was not expecting to get diagnosed with Lupus S.L.E. ...

How I Live To Tell The Tale...

The one person that has had a huge profound influence in my life would be my mom, she went through thick & thin with me because she was by my side the whole time I was in the hospital after I came out of my three day coma.

Whenever I wasn't feeling good she would know how bad it would be, because she would know it in herself.

My life changed from healthy to laying in a hospital to being back in school again, I believe that I could achieve something in my life just not sure what that would be only that I know that I would achieve something. The nurses and doctors didn't think that I would live but my mom believed she did everything in her power to keep me alive.

Graduating was a learning experience from Elementary to Secondary after three months & leaning to make new friends in a new & bigger place, I kept my focus on how to cope with a disease that I didn't think I would be able to handle getting through. An illness & living to tell the tale. I sometimes wonder about how much I went through, my dreams was always to travel around the world with my mom or my favourite BSB visiting different countries or even pursue a career in nursing so that I can help people.

I was never alone on my journey. My mom & the music of my favourite BSB was always with me through everything there was also my dad, brothers & stepdad, any of them would be willing to be there for me when it came down to deciding what steps to take for my life. I could handle any kind of activity that dealt with health, helping others and anything to do with teamwork, I could do anything that dealt with the indoors and handwork.

- Prednisone
- Lisinopril
- Milk of Magnesia
- Calcium
- Domperidone
- D-Vi-Sol
- Nystatin
- Losec (Omeprazole)
- Lovenox (Enoxaparin)
- Imuran
- Didrocal (Etidronate)
- Iron (Ferrous Gluconate)
- Folic Acid
- Tinzaparin
- Methotrexate
- Vitamin D
- Sintrom (Nicoumalone)
- Coumadin
- Kayexalate (Glucose Polymer Powder 94%)
- Vitamin K1 (Phytonadione)
- Zophrane (Ondansetron)
- Ciprofloxacin
- Azathioprine
- Nadolol

Diary Entries

Now onto my Diary entry's, some are long and some are short, but they are all my thoughts of how I felt, and the dreams that I had....Enjoy!!!!

June 11, 2003
Dear Dad
    I wish you could come and see me, because I really, really miss you. I don't even know what to get you for Father's Day. How much longer until you get your green card, because I really want to see you.

June 11, 2003
Dear Diary,
    Hey its 11:11pm and I am really angry because of my stupid damn disease, I have to live with this disease for my whole life and I hate it. I just feel like I want to die sometimes, oh god or dad please help me get through this. If only I would have never stayed with my caretaker, my life would have been just fine without her, if only I would have never went back to that small town where I grew up.

June 12, 2003
Dear Diary
    Good morning, its 9:12am I had this weird dream last night, I won't explain because its too complicated. I am still angry about my disease because I have to worry about my feeding every damn night, and I hate waking up with the damn machine beeping in my ear, I feel like I did something wrong in my life of sixteen. I mean what did I do? If only I

would have eaten more when I was sick in the hospital, but that's in they could of made the food smell better.

June 12, 2003
Dear Diary,
   Good afternoon its 2:40pm and I am so damn thirsty and I can't drink any juice. Oh well might as well drink ice water instead. If only I could keep my food down when I eat everything then I wouldn't have to have this stupid tube feed at night. I so want to get out of the house like my brother does pretty well everyday. If only the people from school could get out soon so that I can see them for summer vacation. I can't wait until summer vacation because I might get to see my best friends.

June 12, 2003
Dear Diary,
   Good evening and good night its 10:35pm and I am not tired at all, now if only dad is around for me to talk to because I miss him so much. Hopefully Kaitlyn would be allowed to come over this Sunday, because I really want to have someone to talk to my age. What I want to right now is to see Ryan and Annie because I miss them so much, but if only school would be out quicker and faster, if only they would be able to come down to see me. And I want to see both Kaitlyn and Christina too, because their my friends too you know.

June13, 2003

Dear Diary,

Good morning its 10:06am and I just had breakfast, I have absolutely no idea what I am going to do today. Maybe I'll call Christina later to see if she wants to come over or if she is allowed to come over, because I really want to have someone to hang out with like Jamie does with his friends. I am wondering why my friends aren't allowed to come over, and Christina should be allowed to come over because I met her and her mom at sick kids so it shouldn't be that if Christina comes over.

June 13, 2003

Dear Diary,

Good afternoon and good evening, hooray I get to go and see Christina tonight either after supper or before supper, now that we're both out of the hospital we can see each other as long as we want now like visiting, so I'm going to have a nap now and wake up and either eat or go shopping with mom, I got paid $20.00 today for doing the dishes for a week and now I have $100.00 in my own bank account, oh and I mailed a letter to my dad today hopefully he gets it on Father's Day and likes the card that I got him.

June 13, 2003

Dear Diary,

Hello! I got to see Christina today after supper, and I just had to tell her about how I earn money by doing dishes and her she does for free, and I don't feel too bad about letting her read this diary because she has Lupus too except not as bad, and its 10:52pm right now and I am stuck with my stupid tube feed which I really hate but I'm keeping myself busy and occupied by watching the cooking channel, the Food Network, yummy I think.

June 14, 2003
Dear Diary,
Good morning its 9:25am and I just finished drinking a chocolate milk which half sucked because I hate the cocoa powder stuff with lactose free milk but hey what can you do, I had a fun time with Christina yesterday she has a car, and it is so cool, she even gave me a ride around the parking lot, the car is blue, its her favorite color and my brother's favorite color to of course. I have a bad feeling that every time I ask Kaitlyn about Sunday, she would just goes offline as if she doesn't want to talk to me anymore.

June 14, 2003
Dear Diary,
Good evening and good night its 10:38pn, I was able to get away with not having any needle or feed tonight, oh and daddy called me today thank god I almost thought he would have forgotten about me. I hope I get to see Christina again soon, because since I've seen at her work I couldn't stop thinking about her, I really miss her. I'm really hoping Christina will be able to come over and visit, because I really want to see her again. I'm really hoping school will be out soon, because I really want to see Christina again.

June 15, 2003
Dear Diary,

Good morning its 9:25am and Happy Father's Day to Dad and Tom unfortunately Tom is working today so is mom so I'm stuck at home being sad and half bored all at the same time all over again. I hope I talk to Christina again on MSN because I have no one else to talk to except Jamie and Bobby which are both asleep and can talk to absolutely nobody for the time being and I'm hungry so I think I'll make myself a moon-egg for breakfast so got to go , I'll write again later.

June 24, 2003
Dear Diary,

Its been awhile since I have written but now its almost 10:30pm, and I am hoping that tomorrow goes by very fast, because I really want to see Christina again, right now I can't stop thinking of a few people Maxine, Ryan, Annie, my caretaker, Jamie and Bobby, and my mom and dad too of course. I remember a statement that Jamie a long time ago before I was sick he said" I wish I was closer to you ", and I don't think he remembers that because of his stupid car accident which really upsets me sometimes.

June 30, 2003
Dear Diary,

It is now 11:50pm and I feel down right upset right now because as I feel like my family doesn't know me very well, I feel like they don't want even want to be near me any more, and I don't know if it's the way I look or the way I act. Whenever I'm like in the same room or something I just think that whoever is in the room doesn't want me around them, I feel like I'm an outsider almost practically every day or something I sometimes feel like I don't live in this family no more.

July 9, 2003
Dear Diary,
It is now 10:50pm and I just got off the computer with Krissy, it sounds as if she can't see me anymore, and I know she has other best friends to but that doesn't mean she has to leave me out of the picture, because all I want to do is hang out like my bro Jamie does, but how can I when nobody wants to come and see or visit me. And she is going to the movies with her bro and best friend and I could that she didn't have time the slightest thought of asking or inviting me to come along.

July 10, 2003
Dear Diary,
It is now 10:24pm and I just got off the computer with Kaitlyn and she is finally able to come over on Saturday and spend the afternoon with me. And like I said on the computer I'm so excited to see her that I don't know if I'll be able to sleep tonight but I can't worry I'll read myself to sleep tonight. I finally get to see Kaitlyn for the first time after I last saw her in the hospital in the Royal Victoria Hospital.

July 19, 2003
Dear Diary,

It is now 10:48pm and I can't believe this Kaitlyn is coming over again I am so excited, and I am so excited again because she is going to sleep over tomorrow night, its going to be so cool to have her spend the night. Oh and as for the family union picnic I didn't go because I went shopping with my mom and her girlfriend. I am so excited I can't wait until tomorrow I get to see Kaitlyn again, hopefully we'll get to spend more time together HOORAY.

July 20, 2003
Dear Diary,

It is now 11:57pm and I have never been so tired and depressed in my entire life, because Kaitlyn was not allowed to damn come over because her mom wouldn't drive her over to my house, I don't know why her mom wouldn't let Kaitlyn come to the movies with me and sleep over at my house, if only her horse back riding lessons weren't so important she would have been able to come over plus spend the night at my house tonight boohoo!

Aug 3, 2003
Dear Diary,

It is now 10:47pm and I just got back from Cambridge, and I can't believe that I saw this purple school bag with the Olsen Twins names on it, I can't believe I fell in love with it the first time I saw it. The bag is so beautiful its even bigger than my old one and lots more space in it too. Its so amazing, one day I'm looking at it the next day I'm buying. I've never felt so good in my entire. The bag is so cool because it has a wallet that goes with it Yahoo!!

Aug 9, 2003
Dear Diary,
It is now 10:45pm and there is three weeks before school, and I can't wait until it starts , because I get to see Jean and Jessica on my first day of school, this is so awesome. Anyway I got to go because I'm watching Blade with Wesley Snipes in it and I don't want to miss it so Good- Night.

Aug 11, 2003
Dear Diary,
Its if now 11:48pm and I'm listening to my Britney Spears CD, and I think the first couple of lines of the song "I'm Not A Girl Not Yet A Woman" proves what I am, here are the lines: I use to think I had the answers to everything, But now I know, That life doesn't always go my way. Feels like I'm caught in the middle, That's when I realize. I think the fourth line really tells or proves what I am, anyway I'm watching CSI got to go good- night.

Nov 6, 2003
Dear Diary,
Hello, sorry for not writing for so long, just trying to get past, going from career studies to civics, today was my first civics class. It sounds a bit boring I didn't mind. Anyway sorry for not writing for two months, just trying to get used to my new school that's all, a two floor school, two classes a day. Anyway there is one secret that I am keeping from

my mom again, this time its just about calling my grandma again, no it is not because I miss her I do a little bit, but I'd rather call her when my mom isn't home, just so then mom and family won't have to bite my head off or get on my case about missing my grandma again, anyway this is a secret between me and this book, got to go good- night!!

<u>Dec 13, 2004</u>
Dear Diary,
 Hello again, it's been so long since I've written but, I am now 18 yrs old, going on 19 in two months man I'm getting old at least that's what people are saying. Anyway I don't know if I wrote that I was knitting but yes I am anyway I am done my first blanket and I gave it to my mom's friend from the business and it was dedicated to our team, and I am starting on a brand new blanket it's a different color now. Oh and I have some new photos on my wall now, it is an actor who passed by suicide, and I've been recording his shows on TV. The show is called Sea Quest DSV, the actors name is Jonathan Brandis, he is so cute, he is called the computer analyst on Sea Quest DSV it is on every weekend so I look forward to it every weekend. The past weeks I bought some clothes, and today I was at the hospital for blood work and that's it. Oh and by the way my hair has grown back and I am able to put it in a bun and a ponytail. Oh and contacted two people today at the hospital. Anyway I have to take my needle ouch but it's not that bad after awhile got to go bye.
 Good- Night.

<u>Dec 27, 2004</u>

Hello again, it is now the day boxing day and I didn't do much I had pancakes for breakfast and then I weighted myself and I am 49kilos today and mom says I can skip my feed tonight so I don't have to worry about much. Oh and I think I may have a new boyfriend he is 17 and he was born blind so we both have something in common. Right now he is in St. Catherine's for wrestling championship or tournament I'm not sure which. Anyway I think he really likes me he says that I was a very nice friend for Christmas. He feels comfortable talking to me. He lives in Toronto and he's an underground rapper, that's been his job for 2 yrs. Oh and he did have a girlfriend but they broke up six months ago. So I think I might be his next girlfriend and it sounds pretty cool. I even got his name and number and what his background is. Oh and I have been talking to him for the past couple of days now. Anyway I'm tired, I'm going to have a nap. I'll write again soon good-night bye!!

<u>Jan 24, 2005</u>
Dear Diary,

Hello again it is 10:53, and I am not feeling good at all. I have a cold and a stuffy nose and I am worried that Herv doesn't want to talk to me anymore because I haven't been able to get a hold of him for the past few days. Oh and I am going to the hospital on Wednesday and I think I might be staying for a few days but I'm not sure yet I would have to wait and see first. Anyway I am going to bed soon & I will be writing again soon. Good night. Bye!!

Feb 25, 2005

Dear Diary,

Hello again, I don't know what time it is because the battery in my watch died on Monday night, it just stopped when I was watching TV. Anyway yesterday I called the G.I. Nutrition Clinic and talked to a nurse about my G-Tube issue and she said I'll be able to get my tube out. Today I called my new Doctor to ask him if he still would me to take my tube out, he said he wanted it out, but I just wanted to triple check if he still wants me to take it out. If he does I can get it arranged to be done got to go bye!!

March 12, 2005

I had blood work done, it was done on my right ankle, and it hurt like hell but I pulled through it. I went to the bathroom then went back to sleep, got up at 8:30 had breakfast, cream of wheat with milk & brown sugar & chocolate ensure. I ate and drank half of each then had a rest, because my stomach didn't feel well. Then I got up and looked for my nurse to tell her that I needed a shower. I had lunch at 11:55, I had tomato soup, I ate most of it, in the middle of lunch a Doctor came in to talk to me and I told them about how I felt about being poked 7x yesterday for blood work then he gave me 2 options either keep getting poked or I would have to get a pick line put in. So I going to try and find the doctor and tell him that I want a pick line put in & I have had a pick line put in before, so I guess I wouldn't mind having another one put in. Then after I ate lunch Steve Scott came to visit for a few hours, he gave me his & Lindsay's cell numbers in case I get bored and want to talk about stuff. On Thursday I came in to the emergency & stayed from 9 to 10 or 10:30 then came up to the 8th floor, 8B Fell that's what its called. All day Thursday I wasn't able to eat anything except ice chips and drink ice cold water that's about it. They did let me eat the next day Friday, I had soup for breakfast, lunch & dinner. And I have already wrote about today. Oh and Bobby came by with Samantha & our Top Gun Trophy & bought me a gift & I got to keep Samantha's last bit of halls & her scarf to accessorize my clothing, this happened last night, I had a great time until I had to get blood work done that was absolutely not fun at all. I just got back from weighing myself and I gained 2½ kilos so 46.5 kilos, and mom said it was just the fluid that they are putting through my pick line it's not my real weight, it's a bummer but oh well. I just got off of the phone with Jamie he was making pizza the store bought kind, I kind of caught him in the middle of lunch other than that he wasn't doing much. Bobby is coming to visit for a couple of hours even though I'm not getting a pick line his coming anyways. I just talked to the Doctors and he said they are minimizing the pokes for blood work to 2 a day so it won't be that bad. Right now I'm just waiting for dinner to come. I just finished eating dinner, it was puree carrot soup & I ate a bit of orange jell-o & I drank a bit of the grape juice, and that is all I can say about dinner. Bobby just left with Samantha, we watched a movie "Ong-Bak- Thai Warrior" and its so gosh darn funny. Anyway it's the end of the day and I will be writing again tomorrow.

March 13, 2005

It is 8:51 in the morning and I just told my nurse Joanna that I might be starting my thing because I found red spots on my undergarments last night & this morning. I told my mom on the phone that I needed the rest of my femininities & halls for my throat & some lip chap for my dry lips. It is now 9:04 & I am going for a walk around. I just got transferred up to 9A, and I am now in a private room and no more noise from an oxygen tank or a mask, and I got my own bathroom with a bathtub, I did have cable but someone took it away boohoo. Anyway mom, Jamie & Carla are a half an hour away so they will be here soon. Oh and mom told me she a surprise, oh I love surprises!! I just got this pen and it lights up inside & its really cool. I also got a new game, it's a multi-game tin board, and somehow it just does not want to cooperate with me right now, oh and I got a new writing book, and 2 more get well cards. Oh and mom & Jamie just left to spend the night at the Chancey's place because Jamie has an appointment in downtown Toronto I think then mom is going to be with me because I am going to go getting a pick line tomorrow, instead of being poked all the time for blood work.

March 14, 2005

It is 8:46 in the morning, and I have been coughing all morning, just stuff in my throat, tickling the back of my mouth, and its making me cough so much. My mom will be on the way here soon to keep me company for when I get a pick line put in today. So far I haven't had my pick line put in yet, the Doc's are not sure about it yet, mom & Jamie had just left about an hour ago, and mom is coming back later to keep me company over night. I just got off the phone with Bobby and he is coming to visit for a few hours which is good I won't be lonely before mom comes back to stay. Anyway I got my pick line put in its still a bit tender underneath the arm, but I am alright. Anyway Bobby just left a few minutes ago, we had fun playing a lot of games of crazy 8's, oh and I got my I.V taken out, I just have a pick line and a g-tube. So anyway mom is coming at around 9 or 10 o'clock tonight I'm going to try and stay awake when she comes.

March 15, 2005

It is 9:28pm & I am feeling very home sick, because I want to go home & see my cat & brother's & step dad, I miss my mom most of all, just having her gone for a few hours makes me lonely....

April 27, 2005

Dear Diary,

Hello it's been almost 2 months since I wrote and I've been doing a lot of stuff lately, I was also sick for a week in March which was in March Break. But I I've been out for almost 6 weeks which is good. Oh and about the Herv situation we aren't talking anymore just sometimes, oh and I met another boy at the last business function his name is Andy & he is 15, he turned 15 at the previous function, so I talk to him whenever he is on the computer. Oh and by the way, I am off my injection, I've been off of it for about 3 weeks not bye!!

<u>May 25, 2005</u>
Dear Diary,
   Hello again its 5:20pm on a Wednesday afternoon, I just got back from Brantford last night. And my cousin came back with me, for some reason I wished she didn't because she keeps telling me what to do in my own house, and she is close to pushing my buttons to far, and I am happy that she is here for only two or three more days, I'm hoping she decides to go home on Friday got to go bye!!

<u>May 31, 2005</u>
   Hello its 11:25pm on a Tuesday evening, and you will not believe who I have been talking to for the past 4 days. It all started on Friday night in a Jesse chat room, I met this girl named Nicole. I don't know what her last name is but anyway, she lives in Oklahoma, and you won't believe what I am about to say next she is a good friend of the actual Jesse McCartney and he is such a nice guy & he is an actor/ sing/song writer. To tell you the truth I keep on getting either cold feet or a hot sweats, he is so amazing. Bye!!

<u>June 28, 2005</u>
Dear Diary,
   Hello it is 8:58pm on a Tuesday evening, I am watching an old Christmas home video that Tom recorded on tape, it was from 2002, the year that I was in the hospital for Christmas that year. Oh and I have a huge surprise for you, I got my feeding tube taken out 3 weeks ago, on Monday June the 6, 05. And won't believe this I get to go on a cruise this yr with my parents, oh and I am going to be with going

to Laos in October, depending on how mom wants to stay there for. Got to go.

Bye!!

July 24, 2005
Dear Diary,
Hello it is 6:14 on a Friday morning, and 2 days ago I got the most horrible news from the Immunology doctor. He explained that I may have a very low immune system, and I am scared out of my mind I just hope I don't die before I'm 30 yrs old. Right now I'm waiting for my mom to get up because she is going to take me to the family doctor I was just thinking just go straight to the hospital. Anyway I'm getting a bit light headed I'll write again soon bye....!!!!

July 29, 2005
Dear Diary,
Hello again it is 12:10pm in the afternoon. And I am doing better, my fever has gone down but I am confined to my room for a few days, and the worst part is I am not allowed to hug my family anymore because I am much more proned to getting very sick easily. I'll write again soon...Bye!!!!

P.S. By the way I never did go to the hospital where most sick people would go, boy am I ever glad I'm not there right now, or else I would really be sick!!!!

Aug 25, 2005
Dear Diary,

Hello again its been almost a month since I last wrote, it is 11:11am in the morning. I am at the store working, we took the store over 2 weeks ago. Right now we are just going through a transition of renaming the store from R & M Foods to A & J Foods. Tomorrow I will be leaving at 5am to go to the airport because I am going on a cruise for a week with my parents. I will be back on the 3rd or 4th of sept, I am very excited. But right now I am bored out of my mind, but anyway I will write again soon......bye.

Bon voyage!!

Sept 2, 2005

Hello again it is 11:06am in the morning, I am still in the Caribbean Princess, I've had a lot of fun all week & I have made some purchases on the diff, islands stops & I've also got my hair braided. I got to go pack my stuff talk later bye!!

Sept 11, 2005
Dear Diary,

Hello again it's been 1 week since the cruise & I'm doing alright so far. I'm back to work now at the store until 2pm, then I have the afternoon off. I'm going to the workshop tomorrow night. This Wednesday I'll be going to Toronto for blood work & I don't know if we are staying there for awhile or what, but I'll see how Wednesday goes, anyway I'm going to bed in a few hrs. I'll write again soon....bye! Good-night Good-bye!!

<u>Sept 28, 2005</u>
Dear Diary,
Hello again it 12:09am on a Thursday morning & I just made my first follow-up appointment with a lady's husband to go to the workshop next Tuesday so I'm happy to say I'm on my way to be a power player & business builder next yr. Going to bed now. Good-night good-bye.

<u>Oct 13, 2005</u>
Dear Diary,
Hello it's been a week or so & I am in Laos with family, 12hrs behind so its like 3:30 in the afternoon in Canada and its 3:30am here is Laos anyway I am back to bed to rest a little more & I'll write again soon I'll talk to you later bye.

<u>Oct 19, 2005</u>
Dear Diary,
Hello I have awesome news, I found out 1 lucky winner & a friend will be able to go and see/meet the backstreet boys in person then in concert but I have to win first. I hope I'm the lucky winner. I'll be rewriting my comment tomorrow because I wrote the wrong location I have to put Laos instead of Barrie. I'll be going to go to the internet café tomorrow with my mom so, I'll write again when I hear more news. I've dreamt a few times of meeting the backstreet boys, I hope that my dream comes true....I'll be so happy.

Oct 20, 2005

Dear Diary,

Hello I'm back no news yet, I wasn't able to go to the internet café, but I'll be able to go tomorrow, I'm going to make sure I go to that concert next week, that is not to be missed, concert Date is: Oct 26, 2005, M.E.N Arena in Manchester, for one lucky winner & a friend maybe my mom & I can go....good luck to me and/or us.

Good-night bye.

Oct 28, 2005

Dear Diary,

Hello again it's 12:46 on a Friday night & have NO news which means bad news I didn't win that trip to see backstreet boys, boohoo!!! I may not have to been able to see them , but I can still listen to them. I bought a double disc of Nick Carter & Backstreet Boys, & also Aaron Carter all 3 are double discs but Nick & BSB are together on 2 discs. Anyway I'm still thinking about the future. Getting my business builder jacket & maybe seeing an actual Backstreet Boys concert in the next yr or two. Good-night write again soon bye!!

Nov 4, 2005

Dear Diary,

Hello it's been a week I think & I have great news my cousin got asked to go to Florida from Quixtar. She is going to Orlando, Florida & I'm going, I'm so excited. We are going in March I think she is checking which month is cheaper actually. So I'm not sure when we are going but it is going to be next yr like I said before. Hopefully backstreet

boys will be there I really, really want to see them, it's been my dream to go and see all five of them in person. Anyway I will write again soon. Bye!!
P.s. I'm so excited.

Nov 9, 2005
Dear Diary,
Hey there it's 9:00pm in Laos, Pakse, & I'm bored as hell, no one to talk to except my bro's & his friend, we are having a farewell party tonight. It's not easy being the only girl in the family because the guys are talking to some girls, & I am around feeling like chopped liver or the invisible woman of the Fantastic 4, but the way I feel isn't Fantastic, because I have no one to talk to there is my mom but she is busy with the other adults. We are going to Thailand tomorrow for 4 days or so before we head back to Canada, I can't wait till I get back home, because when I do I'm going to lock myself in my room until my Orlando, Florida trip with my cousin Vil & I'm excited about it. p.s. so much for having fun.

Nov 12, 2005
Dear Diary,
Hello it's 1:07pm on a Saturday afternoon, & I am on my way to Bankok Thailand on a very roomy bus. Lot's of leg room, back massage & leg lift. I still have BSB & Orlando on my mind. I can't wait to get home, I miss my bed, my room, my computer & my TV & my VCR. When I get back I am going to see if the Hollow in store it stars my favorite backstreet boy, Nick Carter. Then once I buy it I am going to look myself in my room until my Orlando,

Florida trip with Vil, anyway got to go I'm going to relax now I'll write soon bye.

Nov 25, 2005
Dear Diary,
Hello it is 9:46pm and I am sort of depressed because I sent a letter to the backstreet boys fan club and it got sent back to me because of the stamp, my comprehension went to the dumps I'm so stupid because:

1. I got my signed Nick Carter t-shirt stained while I was on my Laos trip.
2. That letter got sent back to me so, so much for writing to my favorite group.

I feel like I'll never be able to meet all five guys in person & get to see what they are really like in real life & in person I shouldn't have ever asked to write a letter to them they probably wouldn't even get it. Bye!!

Dec 3, 2005
Dear Diary,
Hello it's 11:20pm on a Saturday evening and I feel like poop because I just got back from a dinner & dance party, and there was a really cute guy there. The good thing was that he was cute the bad part was the he went after my cousin instead of me. You know what ever since he came to the party I had my eyes on him the whole time, but of course nobody gives a flying poop what I think if only I was smart enough to get another guys email on the cruise, anyway the cute guy at the party ended up choosing

my damn cousin over me, I mean is there something wrong with me anyway, bye!!

Dec 23, 2005
Dear Diary,
    I'm back with surprising news I just met a guy in an ICQ.com his name is Ryan Cujo he is the same age as me and one thing you won't believe is that he likes backstreet that sort of scared the living heck out of me, anyway he is from Japan he actually has gone to one of backstreet's concerts anyway I just lost my conversation with him because my computer wouldn't let me type anymore, anyway I hope he isn't mad at me and you believe this either he said that he loved me (talk about a shock of a lifetime)!!!! Anyway got to go Merry Christmas bye.

Jan 16, 2006
Dear Diary,
    Hello it's been awhile but I have been busy & I just had a fight with my cousin about where she wants to go, she wanted to go to Kansas but I didn't. Before she asked to go to Florida, but she changed her mind damn mind because she has not seen her sister, and she expects me to go with her even though I don't want to, I don't think she understands how I am thinking right now, I know that nobody does. No one will ever understand how I feel, all I can say is Backstreet is always on my mind & everybody that I know doesn't give a hoot about it, I just want to see Nick & BSB again is that so much to ask, bye!!

<u>Feb 15, 2006</u>
Dear Diary,
    Hello its been nearly a week, & my birthday is in 2 days. I'm getting excited now because I just found out that a friend of mine is throwing a potluck party for me at her house as for turning 20 I'm starting to get over acting like an idiot about it, anyway I'll talk later....bye. {{Turning 20 yrs old}}

<u>Feb 27, 2006</u>
Dear Diary,
    Hello its been 2 weeks since I've written, since then I was just thinking out of all of those people out there, would it be possible for one guy to like the of the most popular boy band there is out there. You probably already know what boy-band I'm talking about it's the Backstreet Boys. So I'm curious is it possible for one guy out of all the girls out like the Backstreet Boys, does this mean he is gay, I don't think so. Anyway I've got to go, bye!!

<u>March 3, 2006</u>
(BSB Dream #1)
Dear Diary,
    Hello it's 10:48pm and I had the most wonderful dream last night. I dreamt that I went to a backstreet boys concert, I was in the front row then after the concert ended I was allowed to go backstage. After their first concert that night they sang a few of my favorite songs called "Get Another Boyfriend" & "Don't Want You Back". I was really happy on the inside but on the outside I still miss my mom she is my everything. Bye!!

March 4, 2006
(BSB Dream #2)
Dear Diary,
　　Hello it's a bit early on a Saturday morning I usually sleep in, but I now have a fever. Anyway I dreamt that I was hanging out with the backstreet boys last night, that's right, I was also with my mom along with Kevin, Brian, Nick, Howie & A.J. Now anyway I have to figure out what to do with my fever, got to go bye.

March 19, 2006
Dear Diary,
　　Hello it's 9:56pm on a Sunday evening & I have a doctor's appointment in the morning at 11am. I have found some pix of my mom & I, I'll have them in one of my books & I just replied to an email that my mom answered. Mom was on the phone tonight but too busy to talking to my step dad. I tried getting her attention after awhile but no luck so I won't write for awhile because I'll be stuck in the turmoil of my own thoughts that nobody knows about I'll write again in a few months peace yeah right later definitely... Bye!!

March 21, 2006
(BSB Dream #3&4)
Dear Diary,
　　Hello it's 8:41pm & I have a few things to tell you:
　1. I dreamt that Nick Carter drove me home but I didn't want to leave so when he came to hug me I didn't let go so he carried me over to some grass & layed me down　then he started trembling I don't

know why either, this was a long time ago that I dreamt about this though.

2. Two nights ago I dreamt that I was in my caretakers hosue & there were pictures of the backstreet boys autographed pictures even newspaper & magazine clippings of the backstreet boys. I think from now on I should just tell you about my backstreet dreams that I have I just dream about the backstreet boys. Bye!!

March 23, 2006
(BSB Dream #5)
Dear Diary,

Hello its 12:48pm I know its really late but I had a dream 2 night s ago it was me in a house with the backstreet boys they were singing one of my favorite songs. The song is called "I Want It That Way", I only heard the beginning of the song where Brian was singing the first few lines of the song. Anyway I'm going to bed I'm tired, I'll write again when I have another backstreet dream. Good-night bye!!

April 1, 2006
(BSB Dream #6)
Dear Diary,

It's 12:11am I had a dream of Nick Carter last night, very complicated but I'll tell you one thing it was about the 15 yr old version of Nick & a 23 yr old version of Nick that's pretty much all I'm saying. Good-night bye!!

<u>April 5, 2006</u>
BSB Dream #7)
Dear Diary,
  Hello it's 12:51am & I'm going to bed soon so I'll make this quick. I dreamt a few nights ago that I went into a bedroom filled with backstreet boys posters every where on the walls, now if only I could just find some more pictures of backstreet boys in magazines I'll be able to fill up my bedroom walls with more than 2 backstreet posters & 1 one single poster of Nick Carter. So that's all I'm saying for now good-night. Bye!!

<u>April 13, 2006</u>
(BSB Dream #8)
Dear Diary,
  It's 6:02pm & I had a dream about the backstreet boys 2 nights ago they were wrestling & I showed up & joined in with them. I was stunned to see all 5 of them in my dreams. Then today I woke up from dreaming about Nick Carter he was hanging out with me in my room we were wrestling on my bed it was awesome anyway I'm going now until my next backstreet dream. Good-bye!!

<u>Jan 20, 2007</u>
Dear Diary,
  Hello again & happy new year I can't believe it's been 7 months since I have written last, lots has happened since I last wrote I think I'll just make a long story short as in point form:
  1. (July) Nick Carter that I talked to was actually a poser, stupid people!

2. (Aug) I made my own space from Myspace.com the only reason I made one is to send messages to Nick.
3. (Sept) I found out through my mom that I don't have PCP anymore since I have been clean for 3 yrs.
4. (Oct) I went to Kentucky for 3 days, I went to New York for 1 day, I got to meet Howie D of BSB while in NY, I met Howie the 1st time in Toronto in June.
5. (Nov) I dropped off my volunteer application, I applied for a volunteer job at a retirement home.
6. (Dec) I found out that Jared my crush really isn't going to be with me, I have also met a lot of people or more friends through My space.
7. (Jan) I also found out that I am more "in love" with Nick Carter than I expected, I was able to get his real MSN address through a friend, my new friend is a fan of US5 not BSB but its all good. I am trying to find out what to say to Nick Carter when I send him a message for Valentine's Day, hopefully I can just reason with him. Now present time I am in Ville-Marie I'm leaving late tonight to go home anyway got to go now. Bye!! M. L. A. M. K.

May 14, 2007
Dear Diary,

Hello its 10:03pm, you won't believe who I have been talking to for the past month. I was able to talk to Nick Carter on the phone, I never actually thought I would get to talk to Nick Carter on the phone. Anyway I have been talking to Nick Carter over My space I.M. for the past month I have become: Nicks Princess, Nicks girl & Nicks babe last but definitely not least Nick just recently said that

I am his "Best Friend" I actually became a backstreet boys Best Friend I feel so good right now!!

May 15, 2007
Dear Diary,
I know its late but I have big news, I actually talked to Britney Spears. She said that she, Katrina, a European Boyband & BSB are coming to visit me for Katrina's 18th birthday. It's going to be on July 11, of this yr, I was close to bringing up my dinner just from the excitement. Other than that I have to keep my calendar open for that day or I'll miss my famous celebrity party, no pun intended. Anyway going to bed now. I'll write again soon. Good-night bye!!

July 22, 2007
Dear Diary,
My gosh its been awhile, its 6:55pm on a Sunday evening, I have been busy with posers. Other than that I met a girl that is doing a 10km walk. She told me about it & asked me if I would like to help, I agreed to help out & it turns out her son has the same liking of BSB as I do &so does my friend. My new friends name is Trudy, she is a very funny yet very nice & sweet person, even though she is married with 2 kids & 38 she has the exact same enthusiasm as I do, her son had also let me have his doubled pictures & posters of BSB, I now have a full wall of BSB I upgraded a lot.... Bye!!

My Mom's Point Of View

April 10 2002 (Wednesday)

Anne-Marie did not have a good night, by 4:30Am she was confused about where she was. She had oatmeal for breakfast, apple juice, little diet ginger ale, and they put a line in her arm. For blood work, they put a line in the other arm, another in the neck, but did not work that well. So by 1 o'clock they sent vegetable pizza & red grape juice, milk, apple juice, but she only ate 2 bite and she bring it back up, now that get her egg salad sandwich (they gave her saline at 1:45pm blood was drawn from her at 6pm).

April 11, 2002 (Thursday)

She was started getting confused from 1:45pm last 10mins and by 3:30pm she was confused again and after every hour and then every half that last longer. By 8:30pm she was starting the confused talk. By this time I was awake angry, 24 hr awake, then by 9:30 her brother (Bobby) call she remember him (she said 'hi bobby can you come get me home, can you come now'. Mom open the door.) I tell my son to come to the hospital after work and then by this time 12:45am. She start getting confused and physical really want to get out of bed and I asked the doctor to come and see her, what can she do? Out this time 2:15am finally, the nurse got a hold of the doctor and see if she can give Annie something to calm her down, it only worked for 1hr. I end up get into bed with her to calm her down and she start to say 'mom don't let me go, we are the mother and daughter, I wish we are both before', and I sing her a song (twinkle, twinkle little star and you are my sunshine). Both of us my daughter and I was crying and by this time my son already got there and he was so sad to see me and his sister both of us on the same hospital bed, and then 6 o'clock I have to leave to go back to Barrie to be with my middle son for a school meeting. By 4:30pm her dad came to see her from San Diego she seemed ok for a little while and I was gone to the hospital at 7:30 with Jamie and Tom, to see and we went back to Barrie at 10:45pm and then I came back to the hospital at 1:00pm on.

April 12, 2002 (Friday)

Bring them some lunch for my ex-husband and my friend that afternoon. I see Sandra and I tell her the story and then I tell my friend son and her daughter going to go on Saturday, then I don't know where they are going to stay but one thing I know for sure is my daughter is going to get sicker because her will breaks from both sides that she loves and then she said something bad about her mom and her brother or some kind of insult toward her family, that's why her illness will get worse because she has to give up because she has to choose between us. Where she wants to leave. Because they will not let go of her with happy heart because a month earlier, she asked me to ask her grandma for her to come home with me I tell her I will and then I was talking with the daughter (sat March 9) her grandma's daughter and see if she can help me talk to her mother for Anne-Marie to come home.

But the daughter was mad because I asked her, two days later they phoned me, she had to go back to Englehart because she needs to catch up on her school and then her grandma said I was too busy to look after her and then I know that if I fight going to loose both kids keep my mouth shut for a day and then by Wednesday March 13 end up getting ok with Tracy and I end up telling my daughter if she go is good but one thing she got to do is when she home in charge of her life because she is 16 yrs old if she does not be careful she will die in one year, because I hurt her feelings and I feel bad because I made her feel bad but I had to find a way to get the point across and then afterward I tell all my friend and people I know that my daughter will be sick in two wks and I say those words because I just know.

Anyway by night time Friday night she had visitors from her dad's family, visit on that night, and then she have an ok night and then Saturday.

April 13, 2002 (Saturday)

She was all right but by 2:00pm I went to have a nap because the night before I did not sleep. So by this time the Ray & Michael came to see her and Tracy call her to talk to her and I came back from waking up 4:03pm Anne-Marie was disoriented (confused), and then her grandma Tracy tell her she going to leave Anne-Marie was upset and then I sat with her to help her to go back to sleep, (I thought she was just going to a hotel but she was going back to Englehart for a couple of days) then 6:00pm and then by 7:00pm Anne-Marie waking up and she was asking me (Mom why do I have to stay with Tracy and Jamie stay with you, she was very upset).

I tell her everything will be ok and that night she was having a hard time breathing and seem she has not enough oxygen (air) and then the new nurse came in at this time 9:15pm she tried to give Anne-Marie medication but she does not know how to work the machine takes them almost 45 minutes to get it going and then 11:30pm.

I asked if a Doctor can come and see Annie but she said the Doctor was in the Emergency Room until 12:20am.

I went back to ask the nurse if she can give me a mask for Annie to breathe and she phone the doctor.

She was in the ICU so I went for a break. She can put a mask on Annie's face to breathe 96% 02 she has only 96% 02 in her lungs and then the doctor from the ICU asked the nurse but I've been telling the nurse my daughter does not have enough oxygen (02) she said ok and came back to give Annie (Losec) to help her get off the ventilator.

But it didn't work the only gave her (5).

April 14, 2002 (Sunday)

By 6:30 am Doctor from the 8th floor shows up and he said he is going to send her up to x-ray to see what has happened to her.

And then 8:45am, Doctor come back saying that they been in contact with the ICU to come up by 9:30 that when they went to see Annie, don't look good at all, that her brain had been bleeding overnight and they did all they could to help her she was select and cut she wasn't doing good at all that Sunday night.

April 15, 2002 (Monday morning)

Jane, Tracy & Joe were here and Annie's condition still no change.

April 16, 2002 (Tuesday)

The afternoon her condition gone to worse then the Doctor (Remember words, came to tell us to be prepared for the worse but do not give up hope and then I told the Doctor that Annie should have dialysis on that morning I know about the bran scan all day I went up to 8th floor to tell the dialysis department and said my daughter is very sick she probably need to have it and this night did not look good at all.

By April 16 she was no change but for she was bleeding all her gown, and plus all lines then put in both side of her neck and down below too, and she loose a lot of fluid on side her leg . . .

April 17, 2002 (Wednesday)

Her temperature a little low overnight now 36oc and then she still bleeding on side of her neck.

April 18, 2002 (Thursday)

She start to have peaceful rest, over with out sedation, she only have morphine, and the blood count up little bit and white all up, her protein up a little bit tonight, I visit her at 10:30pm she do ivy a some the morning.

April 19, 2002 (Friday)

I came back at 2:20pm. She is same as yesterday except her oxygen been changed because yesterday they let her breathe on her own with oxygen set, if she don't breathe the machine do not alarm, today everything she misses to breathe the machine will alarm off.

She was continue on through the night and I sit with her through the night sing for her I was tell her that when she gets better we go to Disneyland because in the year 2000 I tell her Christmas 2001 are all go to US Florida, but because April 26, 2001 Jamie as in his car accident we postpone.

So how we do it when she come out and get better again.

April 20, 2002 (Saturday)

She sleep through morning and she did not good in urinalysis.

They will do dialysis for her at 12:45pm today.

April 21, 2002 (Sunday)

My friend and his wife came to visit and tom family came to visit at the afternoon Anne-Marie felt left out but she had a good night.

April 22, 2002 (Monday)

She had her dialysis 1pm, Monday at 9:00am.
I went to get Jane and Sandra to bring her back to the hospital because the rent cost $708.00 and then I got parking tickets of $20.00 Tracy got to pay that and I went here at 5:00pm.

April 23, 2002 (Tuesday)

They send Anne-Marie up to the 8th floor at 12:00pm.
Blood test at 3:45 pm they feed her at 7:00 pm (45 units) blood pressure 8:45-(135-109). Medication at 9:35 pm. Blood pressure at 11:00 142/105 temperature 37.1. oxygen 99 heart 92 Anne got 6 at 10:35 pm bring everything she got feed up with good food caller, her urine at 12 pm-7:00pm 200cc ml 7:00pm-1:00pm 75c 10:00pm, 2:00am—4,000cc.

April 24, 2002 (Wednesday)

8:00am, annie cough bring up green bile, by 9:00am, dialysis but they can not go because blood can not come out the got to put in another line on her neck, and do ultra sound on her arm. They give Annie (metoclopromde) 10g at 11:00am.

*At 10 to 2:00pm Dr for level # 8 came and did some blood test-temperature, and say ok.

They said they will feed her again.*

At 2:10pm Nurse peter came and put the feed for her Annie and they put medicine in the food chop the food better inside, 2:30pm they got to get the line in, dialysis at 5:00pm and they give her dilantin (150) feed at 5:15 pm (20) 10:20pm her urine from 7:00to 10:20 only (18c) 10:30pm Annie she got a care person come in but lose 3.3 L off her blood. Dialysis give her wash clean her up.

Massage her leg, body and in only 12hr she only got (38c of urine).

April 25, 2002 (Thursday)

6:30am, Annie got nice bath, she have a good night sleep well and she keep all her feeding from yesterday afternoon.

But her urine is color green and there start 2 unit, urine creatnine at 11:00am, her line come out 12:55pm-1:05pm everything is fine, and Dr said tomorrow she go to get a new pick line with a double line because the pick line on the left is blood clot, they going to put in the right side of her arm.

I think its going to be the last pick there going to do with her.

I hope everything go to be better from now on because as long everybody stay clear mine be happy for her, then she will be fine and be able to manage her lupus. Because I said that last Wednesday, April 17, that when she felt confused.I hope Jane and Tracy do not talk to her because every time there throw their two cents in to that's when everything seem to go backwards.

I got to go back to Barrie at 3:00pm to see Jamie at 5:00pm.

I hope her dad stay up with her.

(from April 25. 02-April 26.02 everything in a different language, all in lao language)

April 26, 2002 (Friday)

1:00pm sick bring it up bile yellow.

*1:20pm sick bring up bile, 2:15pm nurse give her cortisone.

There kind of medication for 7am and then she went to get new pick line at 3:30, finish at 5:15 pm (we find she lost her hair) she was sick bring everything up when we went to go in we went for 1 hour, she got sick again in the car up stairs the nurse, clean her IV line from medication since sat April 22.

Nurse (Glenn) she check at 8:25 blood pressure 135/99, heart rate 97 oxygen, x-ray at 9:35pm, for her feeding tube medication 10:25pm she get her feed at 11:35 pm,10cc/h take blood at 2:25am.

Oh! Yes today al day I wonder if Jane call and talk to annie on Thursday night after I go to Barrie (April 25), because when I came back to the hospital at 12:40 pm she was very sick, her dad said she have not a so good a night I thought was because I went and have and letter, I found it was Jane and Tracy talk to her not more than 10 minutes, that cost her confusion work up, when get back I insure my daughter everything be fine she seemed ok and so far send her down 5:00pm she was her rest full night now.

April 27, 2002 (Saturday)

3:30am I did not know what they said it was so toxic to her, 4:00pm
she got her vitals sign oxygen 100 temp 37.1.
She was sleep from 8:00pm - 4:00am awake for 5 minutes she went back to sleep again. She got her Big dose of (septra 100/h) at 6:00am.
April 27, she was a weak at 7:00am she yell for me on Monday when Hi! She say I got SLE in my bum Oh! When I look was she have a bowl movement and the CA came in clean her up she was cold little bit, and I try to give her some breakfast but she was bring it up, and she have her dialysis 9:00am, her Blood test too she do very well her blood test at 9:00am was her temperature because (heparin) Medication was in the blood they will do another one they did at 12:45pm and bobby & Jamie came at 12:30pm she was very happy to see Jamie she kiss his arm, they talk and at 2:00pm I went have a sleep, because I was kind stay up all night I want everything be ok by the time I came back to the Room at 4:00pm she was sleeping and peacefully happy, she did not sick and her feed was (20c) hour more than last night.
April 27 at 9:45 pm they took her blood test her feeding ration was around (6cc)blood test 3:15 am Sunday morning.

April 28 2002 (Sunday)

8:40 she was eat all pureed peach, and she very good night sleep last night this morning Vital signs was good, they do blood test at 9:45am Bob's girlfriend at 8:30am and she got her Medication at 10:20am today her heparin for blood thinner at (1ml/h) her saline (10ml/h) right now she sleep but CA came to give her a bath 11:35am they give her 100c water thro the feed tube, she got Heparin (25/a/ (100), 12:30 she eat two tsp of her yogurt and keep, and she watch movie with me, she doing well her color is look good her breathing is good blood pressure 125/74, she was then sleepy

2:15 pm, she got her septra (100/h) sugar level 6.5 at 4:30 pm.

Last night she have a bath, (dilantin 50m/h) at 6:30pm she sleep at 6:00pm wake up 8:30 pm her skin start leaking some fluid again we change her gown at 9:25 she have some chicken-and-rice soup at 9:00pm

For two tbsp, she have a great night she a weak two or three tiny full mouths at a time and she awake the next morning.

April 29, 2002 (Monday)

At 7:30 am she eat little pureed peach 2 tsp eat oatmeal and she get up sit up

Walk with a walker, from her bed to the front desk I take her go for walk on wheel chair at 11:45am we Back by 1:30pm and then she eat lunch so far is stay down she bring up some phlem because Jane called and talk to her dad

2:15pm she sick 3:00pm and I have to calm her down, she have eat some supper on her own at 5:20pm now 7:30pm so far she do ok right now she do dialysis at 6:15pm they put liquid of sugar instead of sodium, 20 mm then they put the right one on, she finish at 10:15pm and after she want me to sleep by her bedside hold her hand and she have medication, and she have a good night and again she wake up at 7:00am.

April 30, 2002 (Tuesday)

She have breakfast at 8:15am she eat cream of wheat bread pudding and shake Annie talk to Jane this moment at 9:30am and then by lunch time she start to confuse and get sick bring up her lunch again at 1:45pm I went out for lunch she got her dialysis at 2:00pm I came back get 3:15pm she was so confused and no sleep at all, I hope tonight she sleep and later around 7:00pm I have to go back to Barrie to do income tax is last day here to send it off, and then tomorrow in the morning 10am we have meeting with insurance lawyer, therapy for Jamie.

May 1, 2002 (Wednesday)

I got back at 3:00pm she is happy to see me, 7:40 (131/101) she have cat scan, her urine 300c for 12hour there can not find anything wrong with her, her blood test is for medication is the same, but she act weird they brought her back to the ICU again to make sure everything ok overnight.

May 2, 2002 (Thursday)
(ICU)

At 6:45am she was talking to me she ask when she going back to her room and she do remember about last night she when she watched a movie with her dad and at 7:15am she ask to eat and drink, 8:15am blood pressure (108/62) (79) 11:50am she got her medication by mouth crushed with applesauce, blood pressure 111/66, they did a brain test EEG 11:30am everything leak ok as I expected, because her emotional, not very her disease act up, and she have another test for the brain and then she will dialysis (her nurse at ICU is Megan) 2:00pm Annie went to get brain test is went well, but by the time she came back at 3:10pm and then by the time 3:50 she still not awake, so the nurse try to wake her up but no response and then 4:20 they got all the doctors show up to see what happened, and then they think she had a seizure, so they gave her Methotrexate 2mg and her they gave another medication for her seizure is still not awake by 5:10pm she is awake now so far she is look fine but all doctor do not what's wrong yes because her test came back is fine so at 6:45pm and she blood sugar 2.9 and then there they gave her sugar in her iv 8:25pm her blood pressure 112/69.

She was sleep again they think she have another seizure there put down the tube in her mouth, now is 10:15pm, there still not ready for us 5:45 her blood pressure 91/55.

May 3, 2002 (Friday)
(ICU)

They did some more brain test again and then she still have tube in her still and all the test is negative soon they want to do spinal cord test again and then she will have dialysis today and the doctor was wrong about the seizure again.

I think they won't find anything wrong because to do with her physiology more then her disease, I went to Barrie at 8:30pm.

May 4, 2002 (Saturday)
(ICU)

I came back at 6:00pm she was have her dialysis and she all ready for her spinal cord test went very well doctor said and there try to take the tube out but she is not ready, I hope there keep it in until Monday because they go to give her one more day of (Methotrexate) at 9:05pm her oxygen level was only 85% I was worry nurse say is ok alarm went off for 3 times in 10 minutes I hope everything ok.

May 5, 2002 (Sunday)
(ICU)

She have ok night sleep I was sleep on the chair by her side that night and last night they start (heparin) and she did not have dialysis today she seem be happy this morning but right now 3:30pm she got her (heparin) I think something to do with her breathing tube seems not right like it has been move inside everything she count her heart beat going up as (146/min) blood pressure 154/100 (4:36pm) they gave her seizure medication (phynobarbitol) at 8:50pm Dr. Ruben came by at 9:05pm, today same afternoon she very tired but they try to get her to sleep they gave her (dilanton) for seizure I stay with her until 11:30pm and then I have to go have a shower because the nurse will give her a bath and then her dad came in after I was fall asleep in the waiting room by 3:00am I came in, she was just sleep then the nurse sent me out to sleep because the might be fore I was stay with her on the chair all night I came in at 8:00am.

May 6, 2002 (Monday)

At 8:20am her heart rate 72, blood pressure 144/89 (110). Oxygen 99, she was awake at 7:30am. I give a hug, at 8:45am take the blood to get tested for the correct blood type. She will have Dialysis in the next half hour on receive blood transfusion, there got to give her (Cyclophosfymide) to do with her Lupus her tube fell out at 9:40am.

She have new (catheter) two way for medication one way to go in & another to go out and right now her heart rate 58 Blood pressure 170/99 (1:30pm), she got septra at 1:15pm she got (dilantin) at 9:30am (Methotrexate) for Blood pressure there got to give her soon there got it now 2:00pm-2:15pm she got her blood pressure her heart rate 70 blood pressure 177/105 (127) blood sugar level 4.5 2:25 185/107.

She was have bowel movement two fine one hour her heart rate 89 131/82 (98). She want me to stay with her all the time her nurse 7:30pm (Angelina).

10:00pm heart rate 79. 129/80 (97). She had bring up some secretion at 11:15am and bring up some more secretion at 1:50am.

Heart rate 105 135/90 now 1:56am.

Heart rate 103 133/38 (100) oxygen 97 (17).

By 3:00am we turn her in her bed and she have a hard time try to go back to sleep, I went out 6:00am.

May 7, 2002 (Tuesday)

10:10am her heart rate 86 113/68 (84) her nurse (Joan), she juts got her medication 6 of them.

I am not sure what it is yet, I know one of them if Dilantin this medication is for seizure. (have to take with no food two hour before two hours after, feed was 8 hours a day)(because twice a day start by 11:00am to 11:00pm, no feed by 9 start up by 1:00) now 11:36am heart rate 86 116/67 (77).

She getting Dialysis at 11:45am nurse (Loraine) she got her feed at 12:10pm (.25) hrs 2:45pm heart rate 87 110/72 (86) Dialysis, done at 3:00pm and will be transfer to the 8th floor at 3:35pm, everything went well, she seem happy she is talking very good conversation good then at.5:00pm she went into convulsions (seizures).

May 8, 2002 (Wednesday)

I got back at 4:00pm, she got her Dialysis at 3:00pm, now 4:55pm blood pressure 135/90, blood sugar 4.2 they add sugar with Dialysis she done at 6:15pm.

I feed her baby food but she can not keep because her throat still swollen at 6:30pm she get her (septra)(iron), 9:15 she was herself again. 10:00pm she got her (Dilantin) 12am she got her feed back up, By 2:00am there got the blood test she got her medication she have a good night, she wet we change her and then she can get back to sleep, until 6:ooam and then she want me to wake up, I tell her I want to sleep until 7:00am we wake.

So by 6:30am she still awake so I let her watch TV.

I went back to sleep in the chair until 8:00am

May 9, 2002 (Thursday)

She got her Vitamins at 8:30, 8:00am the nurse shut off her feed before then got her Dilanton at 10:00am Dialysis she throw up again at 9:00am so we end up restart her feed again because Dialysis start by 9:25am, by 1:00pm she got her Dilanton and her vitamins and then physiotherapy (3:00pm).

Take her to walk from the bed to half hall way (100 feet) she done well and then she eat little oatmeal (3tbsp) and her feed been (45/8) for at least 2 hrs.

Right now 4:00pm, she is back to the room and sleep, she was tired from her work out.

She got Septra at 5:00pm she got eat some puree food at 5:15pm and then Jane call ask to talk to Annie she tell me she just wants to say Hi, but she talk 5 minutes and I can see Annie expression on her face and then I can not hear what she said and she said grandma and then 5 minutes she was throw up, she bring up all what she eat except oatmeal, I think that its enough, I don't want them to call no more. and she hug me say I love you mom and then she get sick again tube come out feeding came off and then she get her medication by mouth, with the apple sauce she brought up everything she ate she sleep well all night from 1:00am until 8:15am.

May 10, 2002 (Friday)

Today in the morning she eat her breakfast 8:45am, she eat cream of wheat, bread pudding three-fourths cup and the shake and she ride the station bicycle for 10 minutes, her oxygen 98 heart beat 156 plus, she have her Dilanton at 12:30 and she keep it down she take by mouth, and she went to get activity, her blood flow in the brain and she if any clots there before seizure, we will get results on Monday, it took one hour, she did well but she have a little pain in the back of her hip today, Tracy call tell me they going to call Children Aid because I ask them if they would like to see or call Anne-Marie at least one month, they did not like that I came here at 7:00pm.

May 11, 2002 (Saturday)

About 15 to 10 nurse came to give Annie medication on her tube.

May 12, 2002 (Sunday)

I got here at 11:30 she was very happy and we have a talk and she do not mind her dad going back to the U.S, her brother came and she was so happy, today I think she is getting better, she taking some ensure shake keeping for at least 2 ½ hrs, she get her septra 6:00pm and her supper she eat about 1 cup of chicken, tomato, carrots, she got her Dialysis at 7:00pm, she feel nauseous at 8:15pm her temperature 38.1, blood pressure 115/95. at 9:25 she got some anti-biotics for her left leg because Dr. Booth think she might have an infection because it was red and swollen at 10:00pm blood pressure 101/63 (76) 37.6, she got her (dilantin) at 11:00pm, she was sleep at 12:30pm until 8:00am, she was keeping everything she eat.

May 13, 2002 (Monday)

She be able to drink some water, she have breakfast all her bread pudding ½ of oatmeal, ¼ cup Peptamen at 8:30am, and she have her medication with apple juice so far now.

9:12am the food still in at 9:30am Dr. Lady 10:00am two Doctor's came by to see her left leg, is still red & painful, she eat her lunch and keep it down, she went for her (ultrasound) for her left leg at 4:00pm, she take her iron supplement by mouth, I was with her for dinner today is Mother's Day, 5:50pm, come back 7:15pm.

She have something for her bowel movement she got her (septra) at 7:45 pm she got her dilantin at 10:30pm, and after that we were sleep right through until 8:15am.

May 14, 2002 (Tuesday)

She eat her breakfast at 8:30, she eat all her breakfast plus scrambled egg (2) and she have bowel movement she take iron, she take her dilantin at 11:30, she eat lunch at 1:30pm the speech therapist came by check her swallowing seem ok, she will order soft food for supper, now 2:17 pm she getting her (Solu-Medrol) she will get her (septra) by mouth internal (iv) (Imuran).

For the stomach 2:45pm now, 5:15pm she eat her soft food, <roast turkey, mash potato, pea, cauliflower soup> 6:00pm, she take her blood thinner by mouth and her Acyclovir.

She bring up of stool softener, today she did not have dialysis there forget to call in hemo-dialysis and today she start eating and drinking now she will retain fluid because in 12 hours she only urinated (100cc) she sleep at 11:00pm up at:6:00am.

May 15, 2002 (Wednesday)
Ramona (nurse)

Anne-Marie have her breakfast at 8:20am, she had a swollen right eye and she eat all her lunch and keep and all her medication, today she weigh 47.6kg.

She got her dialysis at 1:17pm done by 5:17pm and eat her supper at 5:20pm and then have her bowel movement, her heart rate 118, blood pressure 113/79, she got her Acyclovir 6:45pm.

She do not have to get the heparin anymore.

She get (Coumedin) instead, she get (Solu-Medrol) at 6:50pm Peter check the heart rate 115, 118/81 oxygen 99, at 8:30pm she got her (dilantin) at 7:30pm.

She sleep 10:50pm.

May 16, 2002 (Thursday)

She got her medication at 10:30, her blood pressure, start soft food, APO, Metocloprumide and she have good night sleep until 6:30, and she got her (dilantin) and (folic acid) in the ½ cup of water, and is minutes she bring it up all of it.

May 17, 2002 (Friday)

I got here at 1:15pm, she in the dialysis for 2 hours 30minutes, for take it out 3.2L, I think it to fast for Annie that's why her blood pressure was drop very low they couldn't even finish her dialysis, and I ask if Dr can have a look at Anne-Marie.

There give her (Ceeline)) 250ML to help her feel better, she got her (dilanton) at 6:30 and she got her medication at 10:30pm, and she was keep all her supper and then she have a good night sleep, until 6:30am, an then she got another dose of (dilanton) an another folic acid with ½ cup of water 15 minutes she bring it up, now 7:30am she when back to sleep again, weight 47.5kg (105lbs).

May 18, 2002 (Saturday)

She have breakfast at 9:30am and she have her medication for 10:00am DR came in to see her and tell her she doing very well then from there he have a plan for her, she maybe go back to Barrie soon, and she have her bowel movement physiotherapy at 11:00am she walk 200m, and she have no dialysis today, and she have a nap at over 3 hrs and she eat all her supper and keep it and go to sleep at 12:30pm, awake at 6:00am, IV Nurse came in get the blood pressure, 141/115 oxygen 100/85.

May 19, 2002 (Sunday)

She eat ½ her breakfast she take her vitamins and she got to hold all her medication plus her lunch because they got to send her down to get ultrasound done, on her left leg an upper hip and there she have her supper after that she got dialysis at 5:30pm, going to be 4 hours, blood pressure 5:50 150/105 (81)—6:50 116/94 (104)—7:50 111/81 (104)—8:25 111/ 88 (93)—8:50 116/88 (100), 9:25 121/ 85 (98), 9:30 117/81 (93) she got her dilanton 1 ½ (65) 10:00pm weight (42.8kg), (94.5lbs).

She got her Iv back on at 10:30pm, IV Nurse clean change her, Annie has been bleeding little bit so the nurse call the IV Nurse came back put new one, she was have a good night at 11:00pm-6:15am.

May 20, 2002 (Monday)

She eat her breakfast, her iron, she will get her medication at 10:oopm, (cefazolin) and (dilanton).

She got her blood test at 11:45am, she got her (septra 2 methotrexate) at 10: 15am, after the test she was tired because they take to much blood, and then at 2:00pm the IV nurse came in to disconnect her, and tonight she eat the supper and keeping then, an IV nurse came in connecting, back to keep her medication, she say them supposed to change the IV line every 24 hours before disconnect,

connect then should do it, that's what I thought, she got her Phynobarbitol, and blood weight 45.2kg (98lbs) she had urine 800cc, blood presser, pulse and her stool softener, at 8:30pm, by 9:15pm she got her (saline solution) and (temperature) she was asleep by 11:00pm.

May 21, 2002 (Tuesday)

1:00am and take (metoclopramide) and she eat her breakfast and keep, she got her medication on time she got keep off he line at 12:00pm, and blood test, she went for walk 220m, she weigh 45.2kg, (98lbs), she eat her supper she went to the bathroom, 600cc (bowel movement, urine).

She was sleep from 9:30am-12:00pm, at 6:35pm blood pressure 130/90 oxygen 98/ heart rate 79.

May 20, 2002 Monday blood sugar 4.9.

Annie slept well last night but I think she slept on her eye a bit because it is swollen, and she eat little of her lunch, and she when urine 300c plus bowel movement, her weight (45.7kg) blood sugar 6.6.

She waiting for her dialysis in the next hour right now 4:40pm, there so many mix up about Annie dialysis today, they know she supposed to have it but nobody know inside of dialysis office talk to them saying she do to have dialysis today it should be and confused, when she will be next and by the time she go in was 3:50 pm when get in there, they got her wrong solution to give her dialysis, 35, I end up ask them this is the wrong kid dialysis, then they usually so end up there change the solution in the new machine, by then she got dialysis, 7:15 and they supposed to do 4hours now have it done to 3:30 they took 3.3kg, but I tell to take less because can not handle, her blood pressure 124/51, heart rate 82 (4:00), 8:00pm 115/84/84 8:10pm 169/83/94 8:55pm 114/80, 9:25 116.84 10:30pm she got her dialysis blood pressure and stool softer and her (Phynobarbitol) an she got the medication, but she loose 10cc because nurse can't get the air out of the IV line, she flushed with the medication at 11:30pm (one on half lat) and she sleep at 12:00 am 7:00am.

May 22, 2002 (Wednesday)

She have a good night and she look good, she eat her breakfast she got her (solu-medrol) at 10:10am, she was went to walk 11:00am for 223m, weight 43.8kg (96), they check blood pressure at 12:00pm, 118/84 and the nurse (Barb), she got medication at 10:30pm, she sleep well until 8:15am.

May 22, 2002 weight 43.2kg

When I woke up I will leave Anne-Marie IV can undone I went to tell the nurse about it they think I was overreacting but it important to them the right way because can cause infection, he got her (solu-medel) at 10:35am, an then her dialysis at 11:08am.

I don't know if that is good idea her blood pressure 131/99 78 3.6kg at 12:08 pm—124/97 86, 108/82/99 at 1:00pm, 2:10pm—112/83/91 3:10pm 113/84/91, 126/95/77. they take out 2.7kg in dialysis 41.9kg at 5:30pm the nurse say 110/70, and IV nurse came get blood test at 9:30pm because the nurse she forgot to order the test the DR want to see when her test that he ordered of her medication and end up extending Annie line in the small line instead tag line and the disc IV at 10 again.

May 23, 2002 (Thursday)

She have good night sleep awake at 8:00am, she take her (prednisone) 40mg, with breakfast an then bring it up then they give her again at lunch her after she went for outside for 20 minutes and she eat all the lunch and keep it, her weight 42kg (92.5lbs) she take her Kayaxelate at 5:00pm with meal she keep them, and then she have snack insure (the nurse came in to change her pick line nurse Annie name take the old of she end up cut top off her arm skin and bleed little bit at 1:30pm today is first day for (prednisone) she is got sick at 9:30pm sick at 10:15pm they gave her (Gravol) for settle her stomach she got her medication at 11:30pm she have good night sleep.

May 24, 2002 (Friday)

She went the urine (250cc) she eat the breakfast at 8:30 keep her (prednisone) she walk on her own to the shower, and walk back on weight herself 41.5kg (91.2) she eat dinner with her (prednisone) but, she bring it up because she pass urine (420cc), and she have her dialysis, at 6:00pm 139 105 7:00pm, 134/98/109 and she eat again steam fish & rice 8:00pm 132/96/125 8:10pm123/97/124 9:00pm 137/86/114 9:10pm 126/91/142 9:20pm 114/82/107 10:00pm 125/89/90 she it do pretty good.

June 9,2002 (Sunday)

Annie got to Emergency at 4:00pm, stay at ICU, because she got 6,6 potassium and her blood pressure was 90/70 at 1:00pm, and she was tired today because she went to her chemotherapy one last Thursday but it wasn't, now Sunday I think her lupus acting up, they give 500cc of sodium, in case they say her sodium was low 133, and potassium is high don't know what happen, her blood pressure was low all afternoon, now is normal 117/78 (98) heart rate 69, she do pretty good.

June 10, 2002 (Monday)

She eat her breakfast keep it and blood pressure 104/73 heart rate 83, DR to discharge her today go home at 1:15pm 1:30pm blood pressure 87/57, heart rate 77.

June 14, 2002 (Tuesday)

At 6:00pm they took blood test and at 6:30pm she took medication for potassium but she throw it out then nurse give her medication for potassium again and throw it out later on.

Nurse said her potassium 6.1 nurse gave her for potassium again at 7:00pm, one nurse and one helper, they put in her bum, 44.5kg 5.2 potassium,

June 15, 2002 43.4kg.

Going Further Being
Strong & Positive

I never realized how seriously life threatening my illness was, until it was already too late. After meeting a certain celebrity from my favorite group, he helped me open my eyes to how special I was not just for having a health challenge but for how strong I was & still am today after what I have gone thro. The celebrity from my favorite group is Howard Dorough of the Backstreet Boys. My mother is also another one of my inspirations, when I was growing up I didn't know what my purpose on this earth was, if it were to make a difference or something else, but I do know one thing now, I think I have found my purpose. I'm not sure if it the right purpose, but at least I am doing what I love that I never thought I would love before. I knit stuff like blankets for fun when I was just starting out, now I'm knitting for a purpose. A child grows up always asking for stuff that they want in life, I was the exact same way. I am now giving from my heart, something I didn't start doing until 2 yrs ago when I made my very first blanket. I'll be making blankets in the future a lot more, nothing special like designs or anything, just personalized blankets, I just hope the people that I give the blankets to will accept my offering.

Here are my Favorite Quotes:

Still Keeping The Backstreet Pride Alive . . . . Oh Yeah!!!!
(For those who are fans of the backstreet boys)

Never Judge A Book By A Cover
(For those who have a health challenge that
has affected their facial features)

The Bigger Your Dreams Are, The More
Likely It Will Become Your Reality
(For those who want a dream to come true one day)

Once You Get Your Facts Right, Your
Plans Will Always Be Perfect
(For those who want their plans, goals
& dreams to be a reality)

Turning Negatives into Positives

When it comes to negative situations like someone in trouble or being in the hospital, you have to make it into something positive. If you don't act positive, there is no point in trying to get through things. If someone is not well or is in a bad situation, you need to find a way to help out or make up ways to get things seem like everything will be all right. When people say that when they think things are impossible, always remember everything is possible. It might not be at the time you want it, but it will come eventually.

There is a reason why people say that patience is a virtue. It means that if you act like nothing is ever good, there is no reason for living. Being patient or being positive is like doing something that will make someone smile or making a difference. I'm always told that nothing is impossible because everything is possible. You just have to think and know that everything will go right. If you don't, then there is no point in doing anything at all.

I have learned from experience that the only way to get through situations like being in a hospital is by you have to maintain a positive attitude. To have situations go the right way, you have to think of ways to make things go that way. Not everything may always go as planned, but at least you will know what to change or what to expect the next time the same situation comes back to you. When you think you have tried your hardest, there is no harm in admitting that not everything will be the way you want it to be. You just have to try your best to think positive.

Another way of thinking positive is by doing good things, not thinking of worst-case scenarios. Just try to not think of the bad things that will or might happen. Some ways to do good deeds are helping someone in need, giving money to the poor, planting trees to help the environment, and helping kids when they are in trouble. You can also make someone smile by being there with them. There are all kinds of ways to make negatives into positives.

My Thank You To Mom

Kind
Heart warming
Emotional
Moving

Social
Intelligent
Lovable
Amazing
Powerful
Awesome
Natural
Young

I am the daughter of the most amazing woman that I'm proud to call mom, she has been there for me when I'm lonely, she is the most lovable person I've known my entire life. I can say that I am my mom's dream to leave a legacy of love, happiness & smart knowledge to people who need encouraging. I am the one person my mom Loves, but she loves her sons all the same, my mom always wanted a daughter and I believe God wanted to grant her wish because on the 17th of February in 1986 she gave birth to a baby girl and named her after beautiful valley's & fields. I am proud to say that I am the daughter that she gave birth to, to say that my mom is blessed to have me in her lifer is an understatement because I know that once I was brought into this world I was special to say the least. For me being the baby in the family, that gives me some advantages because I got away with almost everything I wanted. I am very proud to say that I was raised by the most wonderful, heartwarming mother in the all of the world. Since my mom didn't have children after I was born, I can say this now that, my mom is a sister I never had, she would spend as much time as she could with me, if she was busy she would always try to make it up to me by taking me out shopping. When I needed her, she would always be there for me, I remember when my brother was in a car accident, my mom was there for me with a shoulder to cry on because she knows how much I loved my brother so much. I remember in 8th grade I won 3rd place in public speaking, I don't recall telling my mom about it, but at my graduation I could tell she was surprised that I won the 3rd place public speaking award. I said before that I was special, I didn't know how special I was until I was in the hospital for being sick with Lupus, I was sent get well cards, flowers & stuffed animals to keep me company at night, all these were sent from people I barely even knew until after I came out of hospital I then knew how especially blessed I am to be in this world because I was cared & prayed for by so many. Now me being 20 and still the baby of the family that my mom, dad & step-father still call me, I may be an adult on the outside, I'm still a baby teeny bopper in the inside. Since I surprised my mom with a public speaking award it was time for me to be surprised because, the morning that she was going to be going to her country along with my brother (the car accident victim) Jamie, they were going for 2 months for family & business. Anyway before they left I told my mom about my argument with my cousin the night before, after I told my mom about the situation, she told me that she would trust me on my own with a friend, like if I were to go away for a few days like Florida, she says that I am smart enough to be on my own. Now for her telling me that I am smart that is what floored me completely. I know now my mother since I was born from her womb, she truly believes in her heart that I can put my smarts in anything when I put my mind into it. The most amazing, caring, lovable person I have ever loved in my entire life. Without this person I wouldn't be alive today, I would owe my life to this person, for bringing me into this world. Now I know why I looked so much like this person, its because a lot of kids inherit certain aspects of their parents. Ever since my diagnosis I had lost most of my memory of my mother, I still haven't been able to gain back any memory of mom and I together, but I can't really do anything about that. I feel bad for losing my memory of anything to do wit my mom, but like my mom said I can't really do anything about it, it isn't my fault, my mom tells me not to feel so guilty, I can't help but feel a little bit guilty. I'm surprised that I came out of my coma yelling for my mom at the top of my lungs, even though I don't have any memory of her. The most important thing is that my mom remembers, every memory of me. During my childhood I had done so many things, some stupid, some smart. Except the only person that doesn't worry about me as much was my mom, because she knows I am well taken care of by my brother bobby & Jamie. I have been able to get back some of my memory not much just some. I'm not sure how to describe how much, my mom means to me, she is everything I love about a mother, she is loving, caring, wonderful, special, amazing, awesome & a natural motivator to others with a heart you can really adore. My mom is my everything, she is always there to help me whenever I needed her, why would I need the world when I got mom to be there. When my mom is away for a week, month, or year I will always miss her with everything that I am, I promised my mom that I would be the best daughter she'll ever have, well so far I'm achieving that goal just working on a few glitches. In my life I can honestly & truthfully say that my mom is & will always be larger than life, as for being a perfect fan I know that there is only one person that fits that title & she is the one that brought me up in this world, everybody knows who I am talking about my mom is my one & only perfect fan.

This is now the end of my story since I am now at the present time, until my next story about how I came to be who I am today as for who my future husband will be, I have no clue until the future come to the present, which probably won't be for another 5 or 10 years but it might be sooner for me who knows I might meet my Mr. Right sooner than I think, like my mom and all the others say "There Are A Lot Of Fish In The Sea" "Fish" meaning (as in Boys or Guys) out there.

Author's Note & Future Career

The general thing about me is that I don't look at all like my age I look younger, but when I was 15 I looked older than my age I looked like I was 23 or something but now that I'm in my 20's I look like I'm 16 or younger. The reason for this is that around the time that I turned 16 I was diagnosed with an autoimmune disease called Lupus S.L.E, I was in the hospital for 13 months that is also including rehab, so from the time I was diagnosed to after my rehabilitation it all added up to 13 months in the hospital, I tried going back to school but it just did not work for me so I decided to drop out and took however long to recuperate. It is now years later, I'm now well enough to do everything that I want, well almost everything. I was just a regular person that had my whole life ahead of me, I thought whatever happened to me when I was 16 would stop me from doing the stuff that I wanted to do, I found out that I did more stuff than I ever did before. I went on road trips with my parents I met new people, made new friends but I did miss my life before my diagnoses. I soon learned to grow into what I had I guess you could say my diagnoses was a bit of a gift because I am more stronger than I have ever been in a long time, my attitude is what helped prevent my outbreaks most of the time.

A good healthy attitude is what I used to help get me through my hospitalization, I may have been in a place where people are sick to get better, I always had a positive attitude about everything. Now when I tell people about why they think that I'm only between 13 and 16 I say its because of my health, my Lupus is what keeps me young, most adults that I meet say I should be grateful for me being as young as I am because then I won't have to worry about getting wrinkles when I am older. I do feel like I'm privileged when it comes to doing certain things. I have made friends with people because they like me for the way I look now, not just for my age or my looks but for me just being me, when I was in the hospital I heard that one of my childhood friends started hurting herself. It had been going on for a few years and when she came to visit me in the hospital, she saw how bubbly I was she is wondering how could I be so happy in the type of state that I was in plus my situation.

After she left she just cried because she was like "how can she be so happy when she is in a hospital?" her mom said "its her attitude that keeps her happy and upbeat". After that she has always looked up to me for being as happy & upbeat as I was and still am today I live my day like it's my last, like if I ever die tomorrow, I make sure I do everything that I want to do before or whenever my day ever comes, I live to the fullest everyday, I now do anything & everything with a purpose. So whoever out there has any type of health challenge, never let people judge you for what kind of health problem you have just embrace it and let it help you, you'll be just fine, like I was told that I was to never let my health challenge run or control my life, to tell you the truth I have used my health challenge to do certain things, I may not have been able to go to bars & clubs and stuff like a normal person does for fun, but at least I can prove to others that I can do something with my life and never let people judge me for who I am and for what I have inside.

For my future career I was thinking of going into nursing, and helping other people. So between going to the hospital, going to school only end up dropping out, I've been able to learn how to cope and control my disease while I am in remission, I have been in remission for awhile now, the last time I was in the hospital was only for a 'check up' as my stepfather called it. If I'm not able to get a nursing job, I can always save up so that I can go around the world & also travel across the country, meet new people and make new friends. I don't know if anyone would think I would have any experience being a nurse, only because I've been a patient in a hospital for a long while, some may think it was for six months, but in one actual hospital is <u>was</u> for six months, then in another hospital it was for five months, then in a rehabilitation centre for two in a half months and I tell you, if you do the math, it is was more than six months. I heard that to be a good nurse it would require a lot of schooling & nursing degree also, except I never got that far in high school I was just starting high school when I was diagnosed with an autoimmune disease. After I was diagnosed, I had spent like 13 months in the hospital, I had tried going back to school but it just didn't work out for me, so I dropped out altogether. Now I'm trying my best to do good in the world. If there is anyway I can do something big enough to make a name for myself that would be really cool. I'm finding my place in the world, hopefully I can make a huge impact in or on the world that I could make a difference somehow. Part of one of my goals is to make peoples lives more better when it comes to health or life or something then maybe make a difference in other peoples lives by my own story, and see how many people are inspired by me, I know a few people are inspired by me but I wonder what will, could or can happen if I can inspire an entire nation or world with my story.

Now that would be something.